MW01596702

Brain Meets World

BY **BEHAVIORAL SCIENTIST**

Editor
Evan Nesterak

Senior Advisors
Dave Nussbaum
Mitra Salasel

Senior Editors
Cameron French
Antonia Violante
Elizabeth Weingarten

Visual Editor
Liam Speranza

Consulting Editors
Michaela Barnett
Stephanie Tam

Editorial Interns
Heather Graci
Anupriya Kukreja

——

Artist
Liam Speranza

Design
Journey Group

Printer
Modern Litho

——

Copyright © 2022 *Behavioral Scientist*
All rights reserved.

——

80 Broad St.
30th Floor
New York, NY 10004

behavioralscientist.org | @behscientist | editor@behavioralscientist.org

We fall in love with our theories and ideas. Inside the dreamy reaches of our minds, the controlled confines of our labs, our offices, our studios, we build what we think are elegant solutions. Yet most of us do not want our contributions to remain forever untested; hopeful, hypothetical, withering in obscurity. We would rather our work be used to address real problems, to further human advancement, to help us answer our deepest, most motivating questions. This means that, eventually, our ideas and theories must venture beyond the boundaries of our minds and into the chaos and disorder of the real world.

What follows is a glimpse into these journeys. The electric, surprising, painful, and peculiar paths that our ideas take—and take us on. From how, where, and why inspiration happens, to the obstacles we face and how we adapt, to the peaks and pains of discovery, to the challenges of mastering the knowledge we acquire, and to the reflections clarifying where we've been. Upon our return, we hope we're wiser than before. But there's no guarantee.

The backdrop for our story is the world of behavioral science, which offers a one-of-a-kind stage to explore the odysseys of our ideas. Here, the author, setting, and main character of our ideas is the same—ourselves.

CHAPTER 1
Visions

CHAPTER 2
Call to Adventure

CHAPTER 3
Road of Trials

CHAPTER 4
Discoveries

CHAPTER 1

Visions

Where We Begin

Look again at that dot.
That's here. That's home. That's us.

On it everyone you love,
everyone you know,
everyone you ever heard of,
every human being who ever was,
lived out their lives.

The aggregate of our joy and suffering,
thousands of confident religions,
ideologies, and economic doctrines,
every hunter and forager,
every hero and coward,
every creator and destroyer of civilization,
every king and peasant,
every young couple in love,
every mother and father,
hopeful child,
inventor and explorer,
every teacher of morals,
every corrupt politician,
every "superstar,"
every "supreme leader,"
every saint and sinner
in the history of our species
lived there—on a mote of dust
suspended in a sunbeam.

* * *

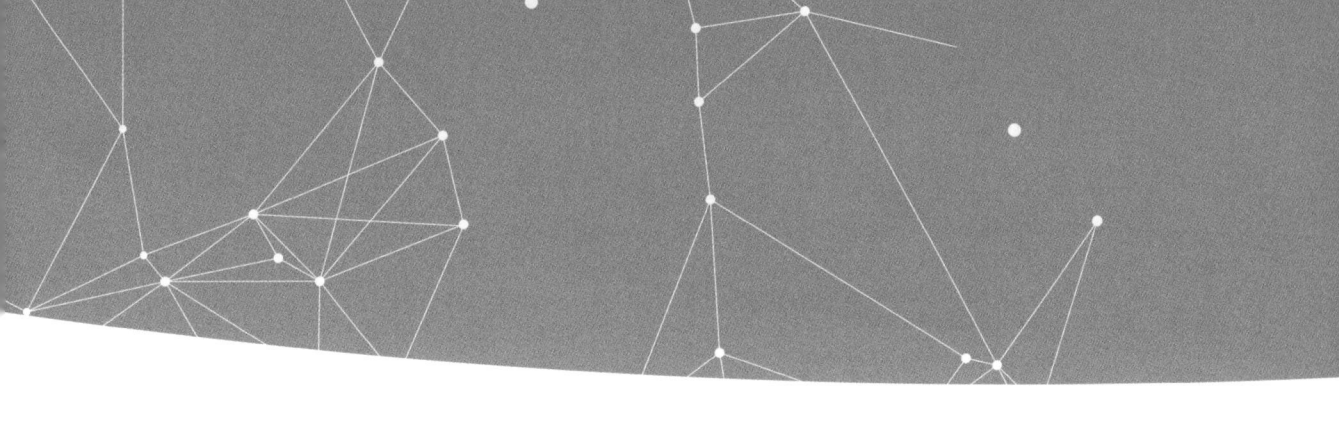

Human beings are
immensely complicated creatures,
living simultaneously
in a half dozen different worlds.

Each individual is unique
and, in a number of respects,
unlike all the other members
of the species.

None of our motives is unmixed,
none of our actions can be traced back
to a single source

And, in any group we care to study,
behavior patterns that are
observably similar
may be the result
of many constellations
of dissimilar causes.

* * *

People are vivid
and small
and don't live
very long—

* * *

This is why I value that little phrase "I don't know" so highly.

It's small, but it flies on mighty wings.

It expands our lives to include
the spaces within us
as well as those outer expanses
in which our tiny Earth hangs suspended.

If Isaac Newton had never said to himself "I don't know,"
the apples in his little orchard
might have dropped to the ground
like hailstones
and at best he would have
stooped to pick them up
and gobbled them with gusto.

* * *

This was what Darwin was trying so hard
to get his readers to see:
that there is never just one way
of ranking nature's organisms.

To get stuck on a single hierarchy
is to miss the bigger picture,
the messy truth of nature,
the "whole machinery of life."

The work of good science is to try
and peer beyond
the "convenient" lines
we draw over nature.

To peer beyond intuition,
where something wilder lives.

To know that in every organism
at which you gaze,
there is complexity
you will never comprehend.

* * *

Utopia

Island where all becomes clear.

Solid ground beneath your feet.

The only roads are those that offer access.

Bushes bend beneath the weight of proofs.

The Tree of Valid Supposition grows here
with branches disentangled since time immemorial.

The Tree of Understanding, dazzlingly straight and simple,
sprouts by the spring called Now I Get It.

The thicker the woods, the vaster the vista:
the Valley of Obviously.

If any doubts arise, the wind dispels them instantly.

Echoes stir unsummoned
and eagerly explain all the secrets of the worlds.

On the right a cave where Meaning lies.

On the left the Lake of Deep Conviction.
Truth breaks from the bottom and bobs to the surface.

Unshakable Confidence towers over the valley.
Its peak offers an excellent view of the Essence of Things.

For all its charms, the island is uninhabited,
and the faint footprints scattered on its beaches
turn without exception to the sea.

As if all you can do here is leave
and plunge, never to return, into the depths.

Into unfathomable life.

"Look again at…"
— Carl Sagan

"Human beings are…"
— Aldous Huxley

"People are vivid…"
— Molly Brodak

"This is why I value…"
— Wisława Szymborska

"This was what Darwin…"
— Lulu Miller

"Utopia…"
— Wisława Szymborska

PART 1

Journey to Robbers Cave

THE YEAR WAS 1948. Only three years had passed since the Axis powers signed the instrument of surrender effectively ending the Second World War. Fifty nations had taken part in the conflict that saw genocide and the first use of nuclear weapons. An estimated 50 million lives were lost and another 19–28 million died in the aftermath from disease and famine.

Borders had been redrawn across Europe. The Nuremberg trials had concluded on the international stage but were still underway in U.S. military courts. The United Nations was still in its infancy. Expansions to the Geneva Convention to protect civilians during war were still a year away. The Cold War loomed on the horizon.

It was in this year that social psychologist Muzafer Sherif began sketching out his vision for an experiment that he hoped would get at the heart of intergroup conflict and demonstrate the means to resolve it. In a letter to his former Ph.D. advisor, Gardner Murphy, he laid out his idea: two groups of boys set in competition with one another while attending a summer camp. Using standard camp activities, Sherif would manufacture conflict between the groups and then set about uncovering the best means of restoring peace. The project would prove to be a landmark in psychology that continues to influence the field some 70 years later.

After two major world wars in the first half of the twentieth century, psychologists began asking themselves what they could offer to help stave off a third global encounter. After receiving an influx of European scientists who had experienced fascism firsthand, the field of social psychology in the United States in particular was primed to lead this new focus of research.

Muzafer Sherif was a Turkish émigré who found himself searching for a home in the immediate postwar years. He held master's degrees from Istanbul University and Harvard University, and earned his Ph.D. in social psychology from Columbia University in 1935. After returning to Turkey following his doctoral studies, Sherif began to speak out against a growing fascist regime, lending his support to the Communist Party of Turkey. His support of communism led to his arrest, albeit briefly; he escaped longer imprisonment thanks only to his brother's political connections and by agreeing to leave Turkey. This arrangement meant that in 1945, Sherif returned to the United States. After breaking Turkey's law forbidding civil servants (including professors) from marrying a foreigner, by wedding an American woman, fellow psychologist Carolyn Wood Sherif, any thought of one day returning to his home country was permanently rescinded.

And so as the world grappled with the aftermath of global conflict, Muzafer Sherif searched for a new home in a country where he did not hold citizenship and where his political views would eventually draw the attention of the Federal Bureau of Investigation. Although initially successful in finding a fellowship at Princeton University, Muzafer spent the better part of two years searching for opportunities for himself and for Carolyn, a search made all the more urgent by the arrival of the first of their three daughters. During the process, he was told that universities weren't in the process of giving aid to foreign researchers. Eventually, with the help of colleagues, Sherif managed to secure a Rockefeller Research Fellowship at Yale University.

It was this fellowship that allowed him to pursue his vision of an experiment that he hoped could act as a microcosm for global relations. Working collaboratively with Carolyn, he led his colleagues (including Marvin B. Sussman, Robert Huntington, O. J. Harvey, B. Jack White, and William R. Hood) through a series of three camp studies between 1949 and 1954.

These camps saw 11- and 12-year-old boys establish tight-knit groups with self-appointed team names like the "Red Devils," "Pythons," and "Rattlers" enter into rivalries that descended into name calling, the destruction of the opposing group's cabin, and even physical fights. Viewing the young campers as mirrors for larger global unrest, Sherif and his colleagues believed the camps offered the chance to understand conflict and, more importantly, develop and test ideas to help unravel it. The challenge became how to put the vision into action.

517 Riverside Avenue
Saugatuck, Connecticut
August 24, 1948

Dear Dr. Murphy,

Muzafer Sherif lays out his vision for a study of intergroup conflict using boys summer camps in these excerpts from a 1948 letter to his former Ph.D. advisor, Gardner Murphy.

The whole scheme of my proposed inter-group tension research is very much on my mind. I worked it out in general outline when I was going through the writing of the group chapter (10) for the ego-involvement book. The facts are already observed (but not satisfactorily conceptualized) on a sociological level. I think these facts bear greatest relevance to the facts of inter-group tension and its grim consequences in actual life. The thing we have to do now is to recreate them experimentally making the variables involved easily traceable so that they can be tapped while in operation in actual situations. The conception of how it will be done is almost startlingly simple: I shall get youngsters of similar group background so that there will not be friction or prejudice initially due to ethnic, religious, racial, or other group backgrounds. This friction, even elements of prejudice or negative attitude of the members of one little group against the members of another little group, will be a function of the situationally created in-group and out-group differentiation or delineation. The whole point hinges on the experimental production of little in-group and out-group differentiations in some daily activity which has motivational value for the individuals in the situation. The production of such a delineation will not be a difficult one - this can be achieved in a number of ways. Until I find my subjects in a concrete situation, please allow me to put it in abstract form. First, get youngsters of similar background (i.e. a background

which will not predispose them negatively toward each other) and let them carry on for a short time a common activity which is of motivational value to all of them, and then split them into groups of 7 or 8 in such a way that the task assumed by one group will constitute an interference or check to the other group in carrying out the activity in question.

I hope that these, as yet, not very well ordered jottings are sufficient at least for you to convey the assurance that I have not been merely using high sounding words to impress my friends that I am looking for some facilities to embark on an important study of group tensions. The advantage of of this study over what has been done until now will be to take group-tensions on the level of group products with the full recognition of the facts of the structural properties of groups and structural properties of inter-group interaction.

While professor of psychology at Ankara University, I came to this country in January, 1945 on a State Department fellowship to do further work in systematic social psychology. I am now completing the last chapter of an outline of social psychology for Harper and Brothers. I am applying to you because recently I received notification that I am considered resigned from my position in Ankara University for marrying a foreign wife. My wife, Carolyn, is an American citizen from Indiana. She is a psychologist, having done further graduate work beyond her M.A. degree (Iowa). She also would be interested in part time work. We have a six-months-old baby daughter.

If you have positions for which I or both of us might be fitted, we would of course be available for interviews.

Sincerely,

Muzafer Sherif

One of the many letters Muzafer Sherif exchanged with his American colleagues explaining the realities of his situation and his search for employment.

The Camps | **1949** Happy Valley Camp, Winsted, CT
Red Devils and Bulldogs
1953 Camp Talualac, Middle Grove, NY
Panthers and Pythons
1954 Camp Tom Hale, Robbers Cave State Park, Wilburton, OK
Eagles and Rattlers

JOURNEY TO **ROBBERS CAVE** Part 1

Muzafer Sherif photographed at the
first of the three camps in 1949.

Jennifer L. Bazar is the assistant director of the Drs. Nicholas and Dorothy Cummings Center for the History of Psychology at The University of Akron. She received her Ph.D. in history and theory of psychology from York University; her primary research focus is the history of mental health institutionalization.

The author thanks Lizette Royer Barton and Heather Graci for their research assistance.

Prominent in the Sherifs' archival papers are examples of the handmade flags and signs the campers created in each of the three camps to represent their chosen group identities: a Red Devil stencil still stained with bright red paint; well-worn flags drawn on cotton scraps proudly announcing their camp and team names; and albums of photographs filled with images of the boys creating, carrying, and wearing hand-drawn emblems of Panthers, Eagles, Bulldogs, Rattlers, and Pythons.

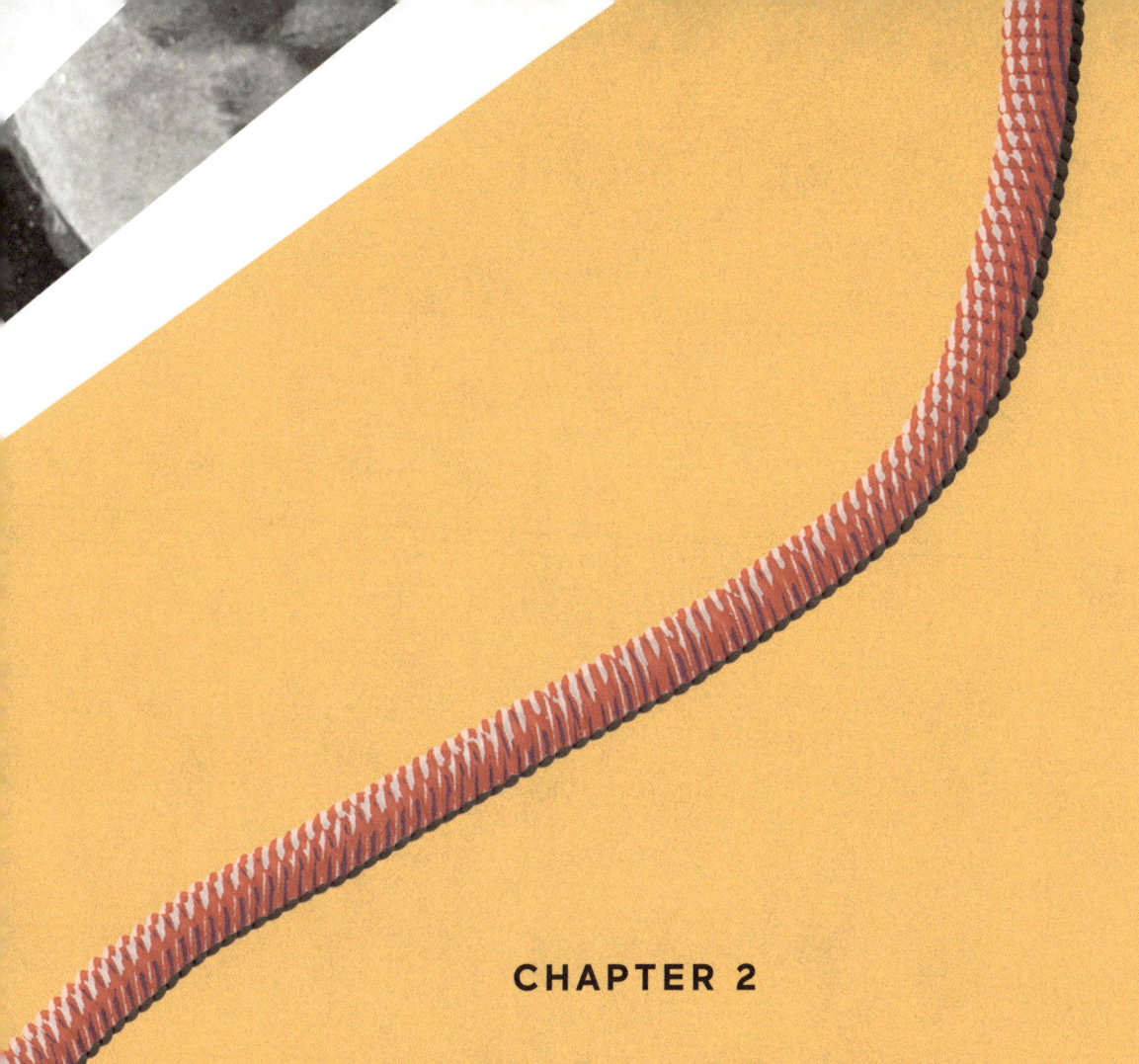

CHAPTER 2

Call to Adventure

"If you understand a painting beforehand, you might as well not paint it."

—SALVADOR DALÍ

Betsy Levy Paluck, The Art of Psychology No. 1

The science of Betsy Levy Paluck is marked by its ingenuity, scope, and purpose. One of her first major studies examined the effects of a radio soap opera on reconciliation in post-conflict Rwanda. In the lead up to the 1994 genocide, Hutus used radio to normalize violence against the Tutsis. A decade later, an NGO was hoping to use that same medium to promote peace. Paluck worked with the NGO to evaluate what impact, if any, the new program—a Romeo-and-Juliet-style story of forbidden love—had on the reconciliation movement.

What Paluck learned was profound. The radio program didn't do much to change listeners' personal attitudes and beliefs on issues like intergroup marriage, but it did change listeners' perceptions of other people's beliefs. This shift in perceived social norms—their beliefs about what others in their community thought was acceptable—did lead to changes in behavior, like tolerating a dissenting view during a discussion. Paluck's work complicated the thinking about how large-scale behavior change happens; targeting processes of social influence may be more effective than the conventional strategy of attempting to change people's personal attitudes and beliefs.

Paluck found a similar pattern with attitudes toward same-sex marriage in the United States in her work with Margaret Tankard. In anticipation of the Supreme Court decision on same-sex marriage in 2015, she and Tankard began collecting data about how people felt about same-sex marriage and how they thought other Americans felt about it. Once the ruling came down, the two kept collecting data, providing them with a before and after psychological snapshot of the impact of the landmark case. People's attitudes didn't change, but their perceptions of what other

Americans thought did. Immediately after the decision, the perceived level of support for same-sex marriage increased.

If any scientist can be said to "conduct" research, it's Paluck. Many of her projects call for skills not unlike those required to lead a symphony orchestra—immersion, preparation, synchronization, and a sense for knowing how and when to innovate away from an established approach to break new ground. She's partnered with film producers in Nigeria to test the effects of an anti-corruption narrative embedded in a film distributed across dozens of villages. This involved shooting a separate scene, randomizing the communities who saw the movie with this scene, and then tracking the number of text messages reporting corruption sent to a national hotline. In New Jersey, she tested an antibullying intervention with over 24,000 students across 56 schools. In the key treatment condition, she and her research team first identified highly connected students, then recruited them to help design an antibullying campaign, figuring that these highly connected students would help transmit prosocial norms around bullying throughout the student body, which she found they did.

At a time when so much psychological research defaults online, Paluck's work stands out for its proximity to life and its appreciation for how life actually unfolds. For her research and teaching, Paluck has received a number of awards—a host within psychology, as well as the prestigious MacArthur Fellowship in 2017.

Paluck grew up in eastern Connecticut in the 1980s and '90s. Her father was a special education teacher, her mother a librarian. She fondly remembers attending the games of the famed men's and women's basketball teams at the University of Connecticut. In high school, she played basketball, volleyball, and ran track. As an undergraduate, like so many with a curiosity about human behavior and an inclination for helping others, she initially imagined being a therapist. But her experience in an experimental lab convinced her that she wanted to go into research. The lab, though, couldn't contain Paluck for long. It was in graduate school, under the guidance of political scientist Donald Green, that she began to conduct the incisive research that's become her hallmark, apprenticing for and then leading large, complex field studies like the one in Rwanda.

I spoke with Paluck over video across two morning sessions in the fall. The first time we spoke, Paluck joined from her office in the psychology building of Princeton University, a sleek and reflective metal-and-glass building at the south end of the campus. The second time we met, she answered my questions from her kitchen, our conversation occasionally punctuated by notes from her flock of chickens outside.

In conversation, as in her work, Paluck exudes a thoughtfulness, curiosity, and optimism that's both measured and infectious. "I think that we get so much more confidence in these ideas—the evidence is that much more compelling—when we see them emerge out of all the other processes that could have been emerging at that time, rather than just isolating one," she told me. "I think that scientists have an intuition that that's what really knocks us down, but our training goes entirely against that.... But this is a *social* science. How are we really going to prove to people that these ideas have any predictive value or a substantive impact without testing it in the sociality of the world?"

—Evan Nesterak

INTERVIEWER

When you have a new idea, who is the first person you tell?

BETSY LEVY PALUCK

It's a little bit like asking for permission. I go to different people who I think will be excited about different things. In the initial phase of an idea, when I'm in love with it, I don't want someone to challenge me yet. I want someone who will give me permission to keep thinking about it.

INTERVIEWER

How do you know if an idea is worth pursuing?

PALUCK

I don't for a long time. It takes a lot of conversations. If it's an idea that leads to good conversation where people can have different intuitions, their intuitions can differ from mine, and we can think of a lot of different angles to the idea, that makes me think it has long legs.

I like it when I hear people say that it reminds them of this or that, because I never want an idea to be so completely unmoored from anything else. That kind of originality doesn't seem right to me. I think a lot of people are looking for that kind of satisfaction. When people recognize themselves, their psychologies, others' psychologies in the phenomenon that I'm trying to describe, that makes me think there's something there—if they can tell stories about it.

But I think you don't know if it's a good idea for a really long time. That's why you just keep talking about it. I think that's also why I don't have a single guru who I go to, I try it out on everybody.

INTERVIEWER

Once you've decided you want to pursue an idea, how do you get started?

PALUCK

I get into the world really fast. I get into logistics really fast. It's a way for me to test the idea. I was trained in social psychology in a more classic way where the goal was to think about a phenomenon in the world and think about how to distill that into a laboratory event. To me, as a young student, this was where all the creativity was sizzling, because it was like being a stage manager. How are you going to put on this theater for a group of study participants so they feel that there's really an emergency? Are you going to put smoke in the room? How are you going to make them feel that they're watching a news program? My master's thesis, which I never published because it really wasn't that good, was right after 9/11. I was thinking about how people were watching the news reports about women in Afghanistan and what living under the Taliban was like. I was wondering what that was doing to the way people reflected on gender inequities in the United States. I was trying to bring people into the lab to have them watch news programming, but do it in a more naturalistic way. How do you replicate when your attention drifts to a news program at home and maybe you're talking with someone at the same time?

I was trained that way, at first. Then, in graduate school, I got to work with Don Green, who said you can do all the experiments you want to do as long as you're in the field. When you start thinking about the field, what's nice is that you get to test out your idea in this reality space right away. No longer are you thinking about the perspective of a person sitting in a white-walled lab space and what that looks like for them or how that feels for them. You think about the millions of different contexts in which people consume news, and you start thinking right away, *How could I get my arms around this phenomenon? How can I capture this in the world?*

So I start thinking about logistics because that helps me to think about specific situations. For me, that's fun because it's a bit of stage management, but it's also a bit of engineering. It's very practical, but it keeps feeding the idea. It runs the idea up against all of the reality. And in the end, isn't it the reality that we're fascinated with?

INTERVIEWER
How did your Rwanda work get started?

PALUCK
Michelle Twali, a postdoc in my lab, is Rwandan. The other day it started raining, and we could hear the sound of the rain on this little metal piece that sticks out from my office. We suddenly looked at each other and we realized it reminded us of Rwanda, of the sounds of the rain on the metal roofs, and we were reminiscing about being in Rwanda. I was telling her that during my first experience in Rwanda, I didn't have imposter syndrome, I was just an imposter.

The way it all started was that, as a graduate student, I was putting together a literature review on projects to reduce conflict and prejudice. I found this radio program in Rwanda, and I emailed them, asking, "Can you send me your evaluation that you've done?" They said, "We haven't evaluated, we haven't even started." I wrote right back, and I said, "Would you like me to evaluate your program?" I did not have the requisite skills yet, but they kept talking to me about it, and I kept making plans and proposing things. I wrote a small grant, I bought a plane ticket, and I just went.

When I woke up in Rwanda the morning of my landing, the chef de mission shook me awake and said, "It's time for you to prepare the training now." And I said, "What training?" I thought I was there to interview some ministers and do logistics; how could I potentially carry out an RCT with these power requirements, and so on. And she said, "The qualitative researchers, they're all going to show up tomorrow." I asked, "Will I be going with them?" She said, "Oh yes, you'll be leading them, and don't worry, I found you a translator. So now it's time for you to put together the qualitative research training." And I said, "Okay!"

They thought that I was there to lead a team of qualitative researchers for four weeks into the field, because they were looking to get responses from many different Rwandans from all walks of life and in all areas of the country on the themes of the radio show. They were going to use the qualitative evidence to inform the writers' room.

So I got on my little dial-up connection, and I wrote to Don, "I'm going to be out of touch for significant periods of time. I will not be in the capitol. Wish me well, I'm just trying not to get fired here."

It was the most amazing mix-up that's ever happened in my life, because I spent all of this time completely immersed in someone else's qualitative research project, learning so much about Rwanda. By the time I was done, I was certain that I needed to do a project there, and I hoped that it could be about the radio program that would eventually come to be. I was lucky that it happened.

INTERVIEWER

I didn't know that about your work in Rwanda. You went there thinking you were going to help evaluate the program, which eventually you did, but this was a sort of prologue; the radio program is happening and you're going to help them collect the qualitative data to inform the writing of the show. What did you learn while you were in this world where science was informing the creative process?

PALUCK

It was the necessary prologue, because a lot of people don't get to or don't take time to do this, if they're doing research in a context that's not theirs. I had read everything I could get my hands on about Rwanda, but all I had were other scholars' interpretations and their experiences. This helped me really form intuitions, personal intuitions. It gave me access to so many narratives, in people's own words, about what had happened during the violence, about what daily life was like in many different places in Rwanda and for different types of people. By the time they had written the show, produced it, and started broadcasting it, I had caught up the tiniest bit.

I came away suspecting that I'd have to pay attention to things other than attitudes, for example. People in these interviews talking about how external some of the violence felt. The onset of the violence not feeling like it was something that they generated but that was visited upon them, almost like the weather or like a new regime.

And thinking about the role of even the geography of Rwanda, actually sitting on those hills and realizing that everybody could see me. The surveillance that those hills bring—there's every opportunity to be observed by others. It started me thinking about norms and peers and networks, themes that have endured throughout my whole career in thinking about the relationship between violence and conflict and prejudice and how much it can be a property of groups and how much that depends on being observed by one's peers and on observing others.

I didn't have that in my head. I wouldn't have known to even try to measure things like that, if I had just taken that proverbial parachute into Rwanda and started setting up an RCT.

INTERVIEWER

You mentioned intuition. How do you think intuition features in your tool kit as a scientist?

PALUCK

You could call it intuition; you could also call it experience or awareness. In psychology, we've made a ton of progress. You can list out a bunch of stuff about the way the mind works, and that's pretty interesting. But now the most interesting thing is what the various combinations are of how those things work together and emerge, or don't, in what William James called the rich thicket of reality.

ideas42 is proud to support *Behavioral Scientist* as a founding partner.

At ideas42, we look for deep insights into human behavior—into why people do what they do—and use that knowledge in ways that help improve lives, build better systems, and drive social change. Exploring innovative, often unexpected solutions to difficult problems, we focus on areas that are vitally important to our collective well-being.

For more than a decade, we've been at the forefront of applying behavioral science in the real world. And as we've developed our expertise, we've helped to define an entire field. Our efforts have so far extended to 50 countries as we've partnered with governments, foundations, NGOs, private enterprises, and a wide array of public institutions. In addition to designing and testing effective solutions that can be scaled for maximum impact, we help organizations develop the knowledge and skills they need to improve existing programs and policies—or create new ones.

Learn more at **ideas42.org**
Find us on Twitter: **@ideas42**

I think that that's where intuition has to come in a lot, an experience and awareness of what is the reality that you're dealing with. What are the complex contexts in which these various tools of the mind, these percepts, decision rules, emotions, how do they emerge? How they combine? What are their relationships? And how do you respond to these various situations? What do you make of them? How do you understand them? And there's just endless possibilities. There are so many different ways for humans to behave. Trying to hone your sense of what should emerge, what is predictable, given these very complex contexts, that's what feels a little bit more like intuition.

INTERVIEWER

In what kind of spaces—offices, cafés, retreats—do you like to work?

PALUCK

I can work anywhere. I honestly don't have preferences. It's October now—I find the fall on the East Coast where I grew up to be reminiscent of school, so shiny new places with clean desks where I can line up pages of my manuscript and mark them up excite me. But I work from hotel rooms and my dining room table and coffee shops. At the office that I work in, I like the excitement of knowing there are smart people buzzing around outside. I wouldn't want to just find a quiet place. I don't need quiet. I like having life, if not right in front of me, kind of around. That's why I guess I like working in coffee shops or airport lounges and places like that. I do like being able to look up and see humans, or just imagine that they're right outside my door, and there are interesting things going on.

INTERVIEWER

Do you have any habits or routines that you follow when you work?

PALUCK

The pandemic has been such a disrupter that I feel like I'm thinking about a different person. I'm trying to imagine what old Betsy did. Two things come to mind. One is that I'm an obsessive outliner. I forget whose advice this initially was, that if you just read every first sentence of every paragraph, you would be able to read the paper. So I like telling the story of papers or lectures that way. I really think about the structure of arguments and papers like that, almost as a narrative. I have to tell the story of a paper in that way before I write it. Then it looks like an outline, and I fill it in.

The other thing I do when I'm writing and when I'm analyzing data is I listen to the same album again, and again, and again. Not the same one for every paper, but whatever album I want to listen to, I listen to it on repeat, to where I can't even hear anymore, it's just a mood in my ears. Albums come to represent different papers in your life, and you can't listen to them again.

But you know, I used to do that before I was a parent, and now you can't really do that as much. You work when you can.

INTERVIEWER

Do you remember one of the albums and one of the papers that go together?

PALUCK

I have this really distinct memory of a Dylan album being released when I was a grad student and writing a paper, I forget which one, to the new Dylan album. I've never listened to it again. I have to be careful. I don't want to burn out albums that I want to live with for my life. I can't write a paper to it. Which Dylan album would it be? It would have been around 2006 or 2007. I'd have to look it up.

INTERVIEWER

Your work is theoretically rich, but it is also in the field. A lot of people might see those as contradictory. What do you make of that?

PALUCK

I think when people hear about work in the field, they interpret it as applied. This interpretation implies that we've reached some solutions and what we need to do is just engineer their applications in the field and show whether it's working or not.

I built my research program on the idea that the way to test and build theory is to do it in the field. We can build a long and impressive list of existence proofs in the lab. I believe lab research, I just don't know if some of the realities that we've stage-managed in the lab occur that often in the field. Labs can be in the field too. It's not the physical location, it's the naturalism of the study setup.

Our antibullying work was one of our most highly theoretical projects, but it's often read as my most applied project. I was actually trying to go after a theoretical problem, and we wanted to push bullying in the right direction along the way.

INTERVIEWER

Do you think there's enough of this type of work in psychology?

PALUCK

We absolutely need more theoretically rich field research. We need more descriptive work in our field. Our field is currently allergic to description. We don't publish studies that just seek to capture psychological phenomena. To me that's the first part of theorizing, and it is a very important part.

Second, I ask my students this: What is the last piece of evidence that just bowled you over, that just knocked you down, that made you think that you learned something about the world? Few people, when I ask them that question, name a study that was based on a behavioral game or a lab setup, these really abstract, precise tools of intervention and measurement in the lab.

I think that we get so much more confidence in these ideas—the evidence is that much more compelling—when we see them emerge out of all the other processes that could have been emerging at that time, rather than just isolating one.

It's the ultimate horse race of the field to see which idea prevails when you just watch people operate in their complicated worlds in real time. I think that scientists have an intuition that that's what really knocks us down, but our training goes entirely against that. There's a role for that kind of precision, that existence proof in the lab. It's sort of the R and D work of social science, but this is a *social* science. How are we really going to prove to people that these ideas have any predictive value or a substantive impact without testing it in the sociality of the world?

INTERVIEWER

Whose work do you look to for inspiration?

PALUCK

I get a lot of inspiration from that really imprecise, florid, complicated writing of an older generation. Some of it is just so completely inspired, and some of it is just so confusing and speculative. But I feel comfortable dwelling in that richness and complication. I'm talking about Kurt Lewin, but I'm also talking about Muzafer and Carolyn Sherif, Solomon Asch, everyone who was allowed, because of the time, to speculate more, and to describe more, to write their articles as narratives about what happens and how people reacted, as well as sum up the quantitative evidence. I like to go back to that original stuff, because it reminds me of where we started before the cognitive revolution hit and brought so many good things to our science, but also starved it of that complication.

INTERVIEWER

When you look back, you see these vivid, rich experiments that seem so real and alive, though messy by today's standards, yet, at the same time, there was this drive to advance psychology to the precision and accuracy of hard sciences like physics.

PALUCK

Lewin was a contemporary of Freud, and Freud's tension system was all internalized. It was all descriptive, and came out of narratives of patients and his own narrative about interpretation. Lewin's reaction—somewhat directly in opposition, but somewhat just in terms of thinking about how science could be modern, how you could take the Gestalt movement and make it scientific—was about not tensions within the self, but tensions between the self and the environment. He wanted to make that a science that could be described like physics.

I think that that's just such an interesting move. It was part of taking psychology out of the individual and putting it into the world and asking, *If we can describe the world's physics, why can't we describe social physics?* One implication of doing this is that we should be a science of prediction. And I think we've gotten very far away from prediction. One way we should be evaluating the success of our theories is trying to predict future behavior.

I think that, in some ways, we've been selective about what we've reified in psychology about how we are a natural or physical science. Here at Princeton, psychology is categorized as a natural and physical science. Psychology sits on campus next to chemistry and genetics. We've reified the scientific method, we've reified quantitative data and replicability of our procedures, all of which I support, but why not also description? Why not also prediction? I think that's a fuller account of how to be a science.

INTERVIEWER

What do you think would help address the larger, meatier questions about human behavior, which are often what gets someone curious about psychology in the first place?

PALUCK

My colleagues and I just completed a large meta-analysis of the prejudice reduction literature, covering the past dozen years of research. One of the ways that we coded the studies was whether the intervention was light touch—15 minutes or shorter, cheap, and easy to implement. By that coding, 76 percent of all interventions in the past dozen years were light touch. And the interventions were largely aimed at individual mental life. The interventions were about training people to control their feelings or to reframe their thinking.

What our review suggested is that all of these light-touch interventions are not getting us very far. The average effect size among all the well-powered, well-designed studies is really small. It's not that the ideas are bad. I think we have good ideas about prejudice reduction, but I think that the next five to 10 years should hopefully see social and behavioral scientists looking toward more structurally oriented interventions; interventions that wouldn't be categorized as light touch, that wouldn't be categorized as aimed solely at individuals' mental lives, creating social change individual by individual. Rather, trying to use some levers that affect the collective all at once to see what kinds of behavioral and psychological change that produces. Some people call those structural interventions. They could be structural; they could be social-structural.

I'd really like to see our social science go in that direction. It would require more interdisciplinary alliances, so not social psychologists doing their thing, economists doing their thing, but rather collaborations, even on prospective, structural interventions.

The next time there's funding to build a new hospital in a place where there are groups in conflict, I'd like to see economists and psychologists, engineers, and so on think about where would we place this, how would we introduce this new institution to the local population in a way that could address questions of social cohesion, and not just address public health and an economic needs.

I'd like to see more of that embedded behavioral science in projects aimed at more ambitious, structural change. It will be harder to causally identify the effects of those projects, but if we can accumulate a bunch of ambitious projects that try to trace out the outcomes of that kind of change, we'd be in a better place, a place that we could be excited about, and maybe expect larger change, or really extend our theories of change.

INTERVIEWER

How do you balance the specificity and focus needed to be a good scientist with the desire to have a wide-ranging impact?

PALUCK

Teaching. I teach in a policy school, and I try to give my policy students that behavioral eye to complicate their thinking. I think that a really important way to have a broad-ranging impact is to train decision makers to think about context, to consider ideas like construal and situational influence, to get them to have that sense of when they should think about a problem through a behavioral lens.

I'm not the kind of scientist that's tempted to weigh in on everything. For me, that would feel like hubris. I am dispositionally more inclined to feel quite certain about the projects that I'm working on to be able to say something reliable. It takes a long time, because every project is so specific in its own right. You have to know well the context and the characters. I think that somebody needs to do that, and that person has to be someone who has the affordance of time and focus. That's not going to be policymakers, so I feel like that's on the scientists at research institutions.

INTERVIEWER

What is the unifying theme or question guiding your work?

PALUCK

If I had to characterize what guides my research program, I would say it is a desire to think about collective social change, not just individual behavioral change, and what levers affect groups of people and collective psychologies—so perceptions of norms, perceptions of identities, and shared attitudes or shared beliefs. It's all in the hope of seeing whether a culture of behavior can change, whether patterns of behavior can change.

INTERVIEWER

What does it mean to be creative as a psychologist doing large field-level interventions?

PALUCK

I think it's the easiest place to be creative because you're actually in the world. There are millions of combinations of situations and people, and the possibilities are so numerous for figuring out how to measure these behavioral traces that people leave in the world.

A great way to spark that creativity is to be present in that environment. If you're going to do a field experiment in a school, I hope you've spent a lot of time in a school, hanging out and noticing who hangs out where in the hallway. I hope that you've thought about where people are getting their media and what people are most likely to talk about. This, for me, is part of the creative process, because you're really getting the perspective of these participants. You're not just making stuff up out of whole cloth. You're watching it happen in front of you, and you're trying to throw nets around it and be there in the right place and time to capture it, or to provoke it. What kinds of events could I organize? What little spark could I add to a situation? It's really a creative, fun process, but it all goes back to just how much you know the place and people.

INTERVIEWER

An artist might consider their painting to be one half of a conversation, and the audience the other half. Do you think that's the case for a scientist writing about their research?

PALUCK

A lot of really creative research designs and creative research measurement allows your readers to be a bigger part of the interpretation with you. For my dissertation, I was measuring the impact of the Rwandan radio soap opera. One of the behavioral measures that I invented was playing for groups of listeners unfinished radio scenes. They didn't know that it would be unfinished, they were just listening. There would be a social dilemma that occurs in the scene, but then it would end. The person holding the boombox would say, "It doesn't have an ending. Who wants to act out the end?" We let the radio listeners work together, and we observed their group dynamics as they acted out the end.

Being transparent about those results and the way that they were produced—describing this process to your readers—really allows them to imagine what they would do in that scenario, or to imagine what kinds of people would play act these particular outcomes. That's an example of something that's a little bit more creative than using a Likert scale, "Rate this from a one to a seven." It engages your readers' imagination, it lets them really think about the people, the place, the possibilities that they could have mentioned but didn't. I think that your audience gets involved in the human processes that you're really trying to track.

If you think about art, it's a little bit similar, right? Maybe the example I'm using is just too close to art, because I'm literally asking participants to enact a theater. But a lot of what we ask research participants to do is close to theater. We ask them to think about what they would say, what they would do, or we ask them to act in front of us in some way.

The more that social and behavioral scientists design these studies to resemble life, I think the more in some ways it seems like art; it's broadly interpretable and demands active imagination and interpretation from your audiences. (That's not to say that you shouldn't also try to benchmark results with some kind of Likert scale.) I think that that's what creativity in the behavioral sciences can look like. It's not unlike art in terms of the dialogue that it creates between the researchers, the participants, the research audience.

INTERVIEWER

What are the implications of your paints or your canvas being groups of people, so to speak? A psychologist is going to be creative with their study design, but the thing they're being creative with are the people they're studying.

PALUCK

This question screams ethics. That's the guardrail on your creativity, absolutely. In behavioral science, as we say, you're always defaulting to something. So what are you going to design away from? How far away does this take people from their everyday lives and their comfort zones? We could have a whole separate conversation about that.

INTERVIEWER

Where do you think the creativity and imagination that you're speaking about intersect with the scientific method and scientific rigor?

PALUCK

Imagination and rigor feed each other. I don't see them as constraining one another. The demands of scientific rigor create guidelines and standards, and then within those standards, you have to imagine, *How could I try to test this idea in the most impressive way, in the way that I feel like I could actually see the effects?* My advisor always told me to try not to do studies where you don't think you'd be able to see the effects. Your intervention should a priori seem so potentially powerful to you that you could imagine observing, with your naked eye, the impact, not just moving a couple of tenths of a point on a scale.

Within these restrictions, then, how do you imagine something so powerful? How do you imagine measuring the outcome in a way that you could actually be impressed? I like the interplay of the two because I think that you can be most creative within a set of constraints. You have to constrain yourself to in order to really come up with something unexpected or different. I think that they feed one another, rather than squeeze the imagination out of science.

INTERVIEWER

What are your ambitions as a scientist?

PALUCK

I have very relational ambitions. I'll be successful if I can look back on my career and see that I've trained a really diverse, creative, multi-industry bunch of academic and professional social scientists who are all over the place working on lots of different things but share this sensibility in terms of what social psychology and behavioral science can illuminate about problems in the world.

I think that my other ambition is to help social psychologists, in particular, and psychologists and behavioral scientists, in general, to think big about their science. To use the science of individuals and their perceptions to think about how that scales up into collective patterns and collective problems. I hope we think big in terms of what we can do with our science. Can we do literally big studies? Can we be really ambitious with it? I think that's my other ambition, to model that, encourage that, foster that, and keep that tradition alive. Because it's not my tradition; I see it as a long-standing tradition that has waxed and waned. My ambition is to be part of that tradition. ■

Disclosure: Betsy Levy Paluck is a member of the Kahneman-Treisman Center for Behavioral Science & Public Policy, which provided financial support to Behavioral Scientist *as a supporting partner. Supporting partners do not play a role in the editorial decisions of the magazine.*

PART 2

Journey to Robbers Cave

HEAVY BLANKETS, PAJAMAS, shorts, swim trunks, underwear, a softball glove—the items listed on the bulletin sent to campers sound like what might appear on any standard camp packing list. Parents were reminded to label everything they sent with their son and urged not to overpack. As a teaser, campers were told activities would include swimming, hiking, and overnight camping. For all intents and purposes, a typical summer camp.

The boys selected for each camp came from remarkably similar backgrounds: they were Protestant, white, from middle-class two-parent homes, average students, healthy, and well-adjusted. Most were 11 or 12 years old, and most had previous camp experience. This similarity was deliberate. Sherif wanted to control as many variables as he could in order to isolate the effects of the experiment; in some cases, his research team painstakingly interviewed the parents and teachers of potential campers and reviewed their school and medical records.

A key part of Sherif's experiment involved observing the boys covertly. To pull off the ruse, the research team played the role of camp staff working alongside junior camp counselors. The researchers were told to avoid clothing with identifiable insignia that might reveal their relationship to the university and to record their observations privately, without conferring with other observers. All staff were instructed to not show any preference when the boys were discussing plans or solving problems. For his own role, Sherif chose to play the camp caretaker, alias Mr. Mussey, as a way to minimize the impact of his Turkish accent while still allowing him to remain close to the activity.

As they boarded the buses, the boys had no indication that their camp was a highly choreographed field study that would soon pit them against one another.

The research team ("camp staff"), with Muzafer and Carolyn Wood Sherif standing in the center.

HAPPY VALLEY CAMP
Monday, August 15, to Friday, September 2
~~Sponsored by the Yale Department of Psychology~~

Camp Director:
Arthur H. Jette

397 Temple Street,
New Haven, Conn.
August 5, 1949.

CAMP INFORMATION BULLETIN

Camp Happy Valley is the boys camp sponsored by the Yale Department of Psychology. It is located on a forest-covered tract of 125 acres near Winsted, Connecticut, and is staffed and equipped to offer to 24 carefully selected boys an unusually attractive and varied program of outdoor camp activities including swimming, hiking, overnight camping, athletics, campfire programs, crafts, and the study of nature lore.

Preparing the Boy for Camp

Now that your boy has been chosen as one of the Happy Valley campers, four steps remain to be taken before he is ready to leave for camp. First, his camp kit must be assembled. Second, he must see his doctor for a physical examination. Third, his parents or guardian must give consent to his going to camp. Fourth, the camp fee must be paid. These steps will be discussed in order below.

What to Bring to Camp

The list which follows indicates what kinds of clothing and equipment are practical for use at camp. In the middle of the camp period, soiled clothing will be sent to the laundry at the Camp's expense, so that only enough clean clothing for 11-12 days will be required.

Sleeping Things:

   3 heavy blankets, or equivalent
   pillow
   2 pillow cases
   3 cot-size or 2 large sheets
   pajamas

Clothing:

   1 pair of sneakers or shoes suitable
     for wear in the camp area
   1 pair of shoes suitable for hikes
     (high shoes with good arches are
     best)
   socks
   underwear
   handkerchiefs
   shirts or T-shirts
   dungarees or khaki pants
   shorts (shorts are very desirable for
    camp wear if the boy has them)

sweater or jacket
raincoat and raincap
swim trunks
laundry bag
Toilet Articles:

   towels
   wash cloths
   toothbrush and toothpaste
   soap and soap dish
   comb or brush

Optional Items:

   camera and film
   fishing tackle
   softball glove
   knapsack
   canteen
   jackknife
   flashlight
   musical instruments

It is desirable that all articles be marked for identification. Equipment may be packed in duffel bags, suitcases, or footlockers (nothing larger).

The camp information bulletin sent to parents of the campers in 1949; similar bulletins were sent for the 1953 and 1954 camps.

Demographic information was collected about each potential camper to ensure similarities across the groups.

- 2 -

13. Health conditions affecting camp adjustment. (Check if present, 0 if not present)

_____ enuresis _____ cardiac _____ flatfeet

14. Parental background:

	father	mother
a. nationality		
b. years school completed		
c. occupation		
d. employed at		

e. check immigrants:

parents

grandparents

Sept. 1/49

Experimental Design ; role of Mr. Mussey.

In an effort to preseve a sense of homogeniety througout the whole experiment, the director thought it advisable, in view of his language difficulty to assume the role of caretaker at the camp. This role , subsequently, enabled him to move about freely and to observe and informally interview boys in the camp. On many occasions he was able to obtain information that was not available to the observer or junior counselor. Boys would come to him for advice or just to talk- his position, supposedly suggested an inferior class position, such as cooks or servants in the home, and his presence appeared unobtrusive in the eyes of the boys.

Every once in the while he would do some menial chore when the boys were around so as to reinforce int their minds his assumed role

Typed notes from 1949 outlining the role of Muzafer Sherif as the camp caretaker.

PRELIMINARY INSTRUCTIONS FOR OBSERVERS (to be revised if necessary)

Prepared by H. Kelman, July 20, 1953

General approach to observations

(1) Verbal and non-verbal behavior relating to four categories (described below) is to be observed and recorded. The purpose of the categories is to help the observers in concentrating on those items of behavior which are most important from the point of view of this study: by keeping in mind these categories the observer will be better able to spot relevant events, as well as to remember them. In recording these events he should not merely note down the occurrence of isolated instances which fit into the categories, but try to present them as functional units, including a description of the process and content of the event.

(2) Observations are to be made continuously, throughout the day. The observers should accept the fact, however, that they will be unable to observe more than a small percentage of all the things that are going on during the day (even when restricting observations to four categories). The important thing is not to get a complete record, but rather to get a representative record of the day's events: in other words, the observer should try to be with the group as much of the time as possible, so that his observations will not be based on limited samples of the day's activities.

(3) The observers are to keep the four categories in mind at all times, and to be sensitive to behavior relevant to each of them, no matter what the experimental conditions. Since the observers are familiar with the hypotheses they may tend to expect certain kinds of behavior to occur under certain conditions, and hence they may selectively perceive these items of behavior. They should try, in every way possible, to counter-act this tendency, and to watch for behavior that contradicts the hypotheses as carefully as for behavior that supports it.

Detailed instructions for the members of the research team concerning their interactions with the boys, the recording of their observations, and the planned stages of the experiment.

A group of campers boarding the bus to camp as their parents look on.

behavioral
science & policy association

The Behavioral Science & Policy Association is delighted to be a founding partner of *Behavioral Scientist*.

BSPA is proud to serve the behavioral science community, connecting academics, practitioners, policymakers, and the public. To learn more about the community, annual conference, and online events, please visit us at **behavioralpolicy.org**.

Find us on Twitter: **@BeSciPol**

ENRIQUE VILA-MATAS

I think a lot about the question of continuity when, for example, in an interview I'm asked about my working routine. I have a theory that it's a question that began to be frequently asked after Hemingway's *Paris Review* interview, in which he said, "You write until you come to a place where you still have your juice and know what will happen next and you stop and try to live through until the next day when you hit it again." The Hemingwayesque idea of always pausing when you know what will happen next caused a stir, and his advice became legendary ... It seems like an innocent question,

but it masks another one,

which is,

how do you carry on writing

when you don't know where

the novel

is going?

Source: The Paris Review, *Fall 2020.*

What Shape Does Progress Take?

Don't assume it's a straight line.

By Lee Anne Fennell

Is this worth doing? The question arises in every domain of life, at every scale, from the smallest and most personal of decisions to the largest and most public. For assessing what—and how much—is worth doing, one useful conceptual tool is a *production function*. It maps the relationship between units of input (like money, time, or effort) and outputs (whatever you are trying to achieve, from social change to completing a research paper).

People often assume, without thinking about it much, that the relationship between inputs and outcomes will be linear, like figure 1(a), where the output rises by the same incremental amount for each unit of input. If this were true, it would provide clear guidance about what is worth doing. You could make a few inputs, study the results, and then extrapolate outward to predict the full pattern, as in figure 1(b). And if you were getting a flat line, as in figure 1(c), you could just call it a day and move on.

FIGURE 1, LINEAR PRODUCTION FUNCTIONS

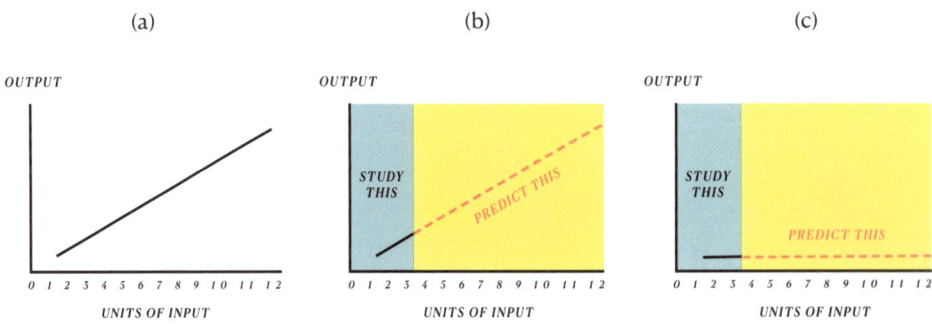

(a)   (b)   (c)

However, production functions are commonly *nonlinear*.

Think of a bridge. If the inputs are bridge segments, we get no output at all—at least not in the domain of "bridge usefulness"—until we have put together enough segments to span the full chasm or river or alligator pit. And continuing to add extra bridge segments after the span is complete does no further good. The production function looks like figure 2(a), a step function.

The value of our bridge-in-progress remains flat as the first nine segments are added, and then jumps up all at once, when the tenth and final segment is put into place. If we were to assess the potential of our bridge-to-be based on the returns we get from the first few segments, we would get a misleading answer, as in figure 2(b).

FIGURE 2, STEP PRODUCTION FUNCTIONS

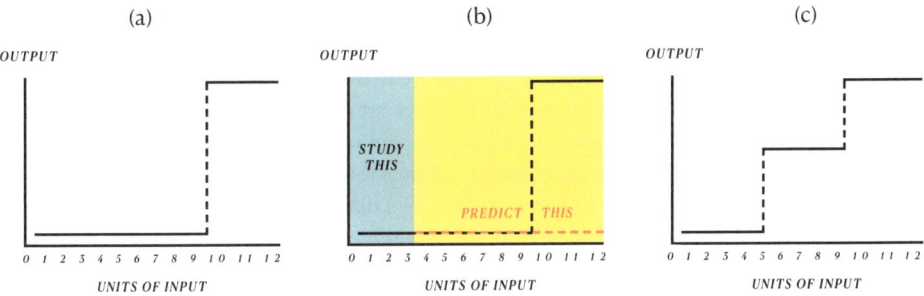

Of course, everyone knows how bridges work, so we would never make this mistake with an actual bridge. But how often do we make similar mistakes in other contexts—in work, in life, in public policy—by expecting linear results from what is really a nonlinear production process?

To be sure, a single-step production function is an extreme example of nonlinearity, one that captures things that operate in an all-or-nothing fashion: a machine that needs all its parts to function, a pass-fail test, or an election result. Sometimes there is more than one discrete step, as in figure 2(c), like making the cutoff for different grades or teams, or achieving milestones like job promotions. Many other production functions don't have sharply defined steps but do have areas of dramatically increasing or decreasing returns, like the examples in figure 3.

Figure 3(a) is an S-curve that might describe phenomena like social movements, learning curves, or the gains from urban clustering. Suppose you are organizing a rally, learning a new language, or trying to develop a downtown arts district in a city that lacks one. Things go slowly at first,

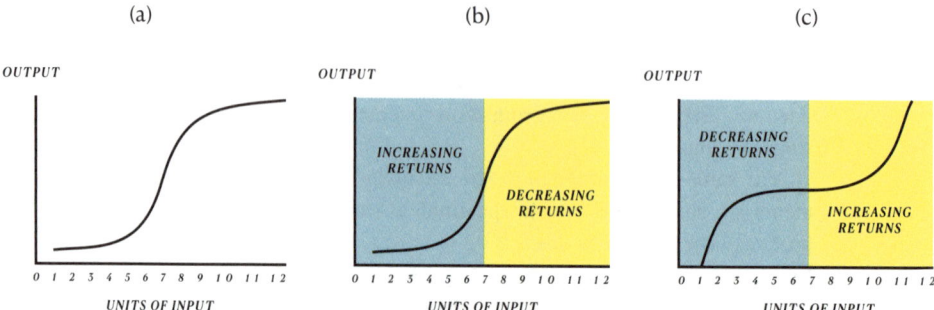

In fact, figure 3(a)'s S-curve combines two different curves, as shown in figure 3(b): an early range of increasing returns and a later range of decreasing returns. Some situations might involve *only* increasing returns or *only* decreasing returns, at least within the range that is relevant to our experience on the ground. Or the regions of increasing and decreasing returns might be inverted as in figure 3(c), where the first units of an input bring the largest gains, then level off, and then begin to gather steam again, taking things to a whole new level.

Many shapes are possible, all of which underscore the error of assuming linearity. Researchers have flagged the hazards of what Jordan Ellenberg calls "false linearity" in interpreting statistical trends and making predictions based upon them. Analogous cautions apply to our own projects, as we determine where to allocate effort and money, when to keep going, and when to give up. Different production functions call for different strategies.

But how can we tell whether we are dealing with an S-curve, a step, or just a true flat line? Sometimes we can't, though careful analysis and past experience can often shed light on what combinations of inputs are most likely to produce returns, and whether those results are likely to appear little by little or in large lumps of value. We can ask ourselves some questions: Are there fixed costs that need to be covered up front to get things going, or a certain critical mass of participants who have to be on board before things take off? Is the first stab at this type of problem usually the most significant, with later follow-ups helping significantly less? Are there good reasons to think that a policy might produce different results in the long run from those that are visible in the short run?

Consider the Moving to Opportunity studies, which investigated the effects of housing mobility and neighborhood environment on families who had been living in public housing. The experiment, which ran in five large U.S. cities in the 1990s, randomly assigned some families to receive experimental housing vouchers that, unlike ordinary Section 8 vouchers, could only be used in low-poverty neighborhoods. The observed effects of this intervention were initially underwhelming. Although the intervention *did* deliver some important benefits (like improved subjective well-being, family safety, and better mental and physical health), the hoped-for gains in earnings and employment rates didn't seem to materialize. But in 2016, Raj Chetty and his coauthors published a new study that traced the long-term effects on children who were younger than age 13 when their families received vouchers to move to low-poverty neighborhoods. These children, unlike their older counterparts, were more likely to attend college and earned more in adulthood than those whose families received regular Section 8 vouchers or no voucher. Longer exposures to low-poverty neighborhoods, starting earlier in childhood, produced results that exposures starting later in life did not. Extrapolating from the initial data would have been as misleading as judging a bridge's potential on the performance of the first few segments. Even when we remain uncertain about the precise shape that a production function takes, keeping the possibility of nonlinearity in mind can help keep us patient and humble.

Nonlinear production functions can be both exciting and daunting. The possibility of a bridge-completing breakthrough can be highly motivating, but the prospect of never being able to put together all of the necessary elements to produce one can keep some would-be bridge-builders from ever starting at all. Often, we must send our bridge segments out into the world without knowing yet how, or whether, they will fit together with other inputs—our own or those of others—to create something of value. At the same time, we must always be on the lookout for opportunities to connect our own contributions to the bridge segments built by others.

These lessons of nonlinearity can also inform our everyday lives and shed light on otherwise puzzling aspects of human behavior. Continuing to pour money or effort into an enterprise that is not generating any apparent returns might look like a sunk cost fallacy from the outside, but may feel like bridge building from the inside. Conversely, pursuing the predictably productive day by day might mean missing out on a larger gain that can only come from stepping away from the treadmill long enough to engineer a larger leap.

Before embarking on any undertaking—and especially before giving up on it—ask yourself what the production function looks like. And when assessing what is worth doing or supporting, or when gauging what counts as success, stay attuned to the prospects of *nonlinear* production in your own life and those of others. ∎

Lee Anne Fennell is the Max Pam Professor of Law at the University of Chicago Law School. She is the author of *The Unbounded Home* and *Slices and Lumps: Division and Aggregation in Law and Life*.

One Small Step, One Giant Heave

By Danny Oppenheimer

Throwing up is always unpleasant. But throwing up in zero gravity, with your vomit just floating in front of your face, taunting you, is much, much, worse. Especially when your feet aren't anchored to the ground and the force created by your heaving sends you spinning in circles.

When I first heard about NASA's grant for aspiring scientists to conduct research in zero gravity, I was convinced it was made for me. An undergraduate at the time, and an avid science fiction reader, my creativity to common sense ratio was badly skewed. (It still is, but not quite as egregiously.) So I walked into the office of my advisor, cognitive psychology professor Mike Watkins, and declared my plan to conduct a study in zero-g. "Danny," he replied, "unfortunately, there's gravity on Earth."

Undeterred by that trivial detail, I convinced Professor Watkins and a fellow psych major that we could come up with something. I knew I'd never be an astronaut—my eyesight was too poor—but this was my chance to make my nerdy, sci-fi dreams of astronaut training come true.

After a bit of brainstorming, the idea came to us: state-dependent memory. A few decades earlier, David Godden and Alan Baddeley had run a classic study on how scuba divers learn pressure tables. Divers who studied while underwater remembered the material better when tested underwater, whereas divers who studied while on land remembered better when tested on land. This suggested that the environment where you learn influences how well you remember later. Nobody had ever explored whether the effect would generalize to gravitational states. If we learn in zero gravity, do we remember better when in zero gravity later? The answer could have implications for training astronauts.

In retrospect, the theoretical advance of the proposal could be generously described as modest, but I think NASA was so surprised by the novelty of an application from behavioral scientists that our proposal was approved anyway.

To prepare to go into zero-g on NASA's KC-135 airplane, we had to go through several weeks of training. We trained in oxygen deprivation chambers and learned how to deal with rapid decompression. At all times during the training period and for a time after the experiment, we were required to wear a little card that said, "NASA Hazardous Duty" (yes, I still have it), because if I collapsed or needed to go to the hospital, the doctors would need to know.

The KC-135 creates weightlessness by first climbing to high altitudes and then entering free fall, allowing passengers to float (relative to the plane around them) for about 30 seconds before the plane levels out and begins the cycle again. During the climb, passengers experience close to twice the normal gravitational forces; during the fall, passengers experience zero-g.

In additional to weightlessness, passengers also commonly experience nausea, thus earning the KC-135 the moniker "Vomit Comet." Fortunately, NASA has come up with a way to prevent passengers on the KC-135 from suffering the extreme nausea that such an experience normally induces: Scop-Dex, a mixture of scopolamine (a drug that prevents motion sickness) and Dexedrine (a stimulant that counters the side effects of scopolamine). So rest assured, if you have to go into zero gravity, you won't have to deal with the debilitating nausea that the Vomit Comet is known for.

Unless, of course, you run into trouble with the research ethics review board (something that only we, as behavioral scientists, had to deal with), and they don't approve Scop-Dex. The ethics board thought that giving undergraduates the opportunity to go into zero gravity was coercive because no undergraduate could turn down an opportunity like that. And because it was coercive, we shouldn't be allowed to do it at all. This was compounded by the fact that my college didn't have a medical school, and so the reviewers were nervous about participants taking any drugs. In NASA's eyes, what we were doing—having people remember things—was not an issue and paled in comparison to the tests they put would-be astronauts through. After much back and forth, we reached a compromise. The study could go ahead, but with no Scop-Dex.

On the KC-135, we set up our experiment alongside the other research teams. One I remember in particular was a group of engineering students who were testing power drills that displaced the torque; if you used a regular power drill in zero-g, you'd end up spinning in circles.

We equipped our participants with noise-cancelling headphones. They were going to hear a list of words and had to note whether each word was new or old, depending on whether they had heard it before. Early on, this is easy, because all the words are new. But eventually, the words are mixed more evenly. The question is: If you hear a word for the second time in the same gravitational conditions that you originally heard it, are you more likely to remember it? The plane took off and the lists started.

Ten to 15 minutes later, after only a few of the zero-g parabolas, I threw up for the first time.

On Earth, what goes up must come down. In zero-g, what comes up, floats. And in zero-g, the esophageal thrust, so to speak, sends you spinning. And your eyes are closed because you're vomiting. And you're trying to hold the NASA-approved bag around your mouth, hoping as little as possible escapes. Then a flashing light comes on indicating you have a handful of seconds to get to the floor of the plane, before the parabola finishes and gravity reasserts itself (remember, at near twice the force of regular gravity). But since you've been spinning with

On Earth, what goes up must come down. In zero-g, what comes up, floats.

your eyes closed, you don't know which way is down. So you're trying to watch other people to figure out where they go, but they're trying to finish their experiments, so you only have a few seconds to get to the floor before gravity hits. And you're really, really trying not to let the bag slip off of your mouth.

After a few parabolas, it was hopeless. Some of the members from the other teams (the ones who could take Scop-Dex) strapped me down in the back of the plane. There, I counted down the remaining parabolas—50 more. 50 more left. Only 50 more left. 49. Only 49 left.

The two and a half hours of that flight were some of the worst of my life. I'll never forget one research team blowing bubbles (their project investigated surface tension of bubbles in zero gravity) having the time of their lives. And when we finally got down to zero parabolas left, the captain came on and asked, "Before we go down, would anyone like to see what lunar gravity is like? We can emulate lunar gravity …"

The bubble-blowing scientists cheered. Why not? Wouldn't it be fun to blow bubbles on the moon?

I moaned; unfortunately, I was so hoarse from heaving that no one heard. So I experienced lunar gravity cargo-strapped to a plane with a bag over my mouth. And Martian gravity too. By the time the KC-135 landed, I had lost 10 pounds.

Only one of our participants made it through the whole experiment without getting sick. In the end, we didn't get much data, though my research conclusively demonstrated one thing: people don't remember whether a word is new or old while vomiting. Unfortunately, this finding was not considered surprising or important enough for publication.

———

Many behavioral researchers do extraordinarily clever things to collect data given the con-straints imposed by the environment. Maybe they're doing research in a country where research is very difficult, because of issues with the government or language barriers or limited technology. Maybe they're testing theories that require conditions rarely seen in naturalistic settings. So maybe behavioral science in zero gravity isn't as strange as it sounded when I walked into Professor Watkins's office all those years ago.

And, in spite of the misery of that experience, there were some silver linings. First, my motion sickness was cured. I used to be the person who couldn't get on a boat, and when in a car on twisty mountain roads would always have to sit in the front seat and have to stop. But not since this incident.

Second, I was hooked on research and thinking creatively about the different ways we might investigate a problem. Looking back, 20 years later, now as a full professor, it was a fun challenge to design stimuli given the unusual logistical constraints. And it obviously didn't dampen my enthusiasm for research.

As scientists curious about human behavior, we want to see whether our findings generalize beyond the lab, and going beyond the lab is tricky. Outside of the lab, we lose control over many things, sometimes even the contents of our stomachs. ∎

———

Danny Oppenheimer is a professor at Carnegie Mellon jointly appointed in psychology and decision sciences. He studies judgment, decision-making, metacognition, learning, and causal reasoning, and applies his findings to a diverse array of domains, such as charitable giving, consumer behavior, education, electoral outcomes, and how to trick students into buying him ice cream. He is the author of *Democracy Despite Itself* and *Psychology: The Comic Book Introduction*.

The BEAR center at the Rotman School, University of Toronto is home to the Behaviourally Informed Organizations partnership. Our goal is to co-create—with our many academic, government, policy, business, and student partners—a science of using behavioral science. This includes an integrative framework for behavior change, applications to financial, personal, and environmental well-being, and helping organizations better embed and harness behavioral science for individual and societal prosperity. BEAR is also home to the popular BE101x (Behavioural Economics in Action) course on edX.

BEAR: **rotman.utoronto.ca/bear**
Behaviourally Informed Organizations: **biorgpartnership.com**
BE101x: **edx.org/course/behavioural-economics-in-action**
Twitter: **@UofT_BEAR**

An Horatian Notion

By Thomas Lux

The thing gets made, gets built, and you're the slave
who rolls the log beneath the block, then another,
then pushes the block, then pulls a log
from the rear back to the front
again and then again it goes beneath the block,
and so on. It's how a thing gets made — not
because you're sensitive, or you get genetic-lucky,
or God says: Here's a nice family,
seven children, let's see: this one in charge
of the village dunghill, these two die of buboes, this one
Kierkegaard, this one a drooling

nincompoop, this one clerk, this one cooper.
You need to love the thing you do — birdhouse building,
painting tulips exclusively, whatever — and then
you do it
so consciously driven
by your unconscious
that the thing becomes a wedge
that splits a stone and between the halves
the wedge then grows, i.e., the thing
is solid but with a soul,
a life of its own. Inspiration, the donnée,

the gift, the bolt of fire
down the arm that makes the art?
Grow up! Give me, please, a break!
You make the thing because you love the thing
and you love the thing because someone else loved it
enough to make you love it.
And with that your heart like a tent peg pounded
toward the earth's core.
And with that your heart on a beam burns
through the ionosphere.
And with that you go to work.

CHAPTER 3

Road of Trials

*"In order to rise from its own ashes,
a phoenix first must burn."*

—OCTAVIA E. BUTLER

Places Unexpected

By Evan Nesterak

It was a clear, February afternoon along National Route 40 in southern Patagonia, a few miles outside a small Argentine town called Gobernador Gregores. To the southwest, the Playa de los Icebergs peered up to Cerro Torre peak, 10,262 feet high. To the northeast, the remains of a 150-million-year-old forest stood protected by the Parque Nacional Bosques Petrificados. Due north, hundreds of handprints covered the walls of Cueva de las Manos, as they have for the past 9,000 years.

And at this moment in the story, our two main characters, Thomas Andrillon and Chiara Varazzani, 28 years old and married eight months, are hanging upside down in their 2006 Land Rover Defender named Bechamel, still buckled in.

The road wasn't in bad condition. They'd spent the previous two days traversing rocky, mountainous roads as they moved along the Southern Patagonian Ice Field and then inland. But the road they were on, emphasis on *were,* was not like that at all. It was smooth, sealed, flat, and mostly straight.

They weren't inexperienced travelers. Over the past six months, Thomas, Chiara, and

Bechamel made it through Europe, Africa, and South America, crossed one sea, one ocean, dozens of rivers, deserts, and mountain passes, and covered over 10,000 miles.

Thomas, who was driving, wasn't tired. Though they'd passed through some rough terrain, he still felt alert. And, besides, they only had a few more miles to go.

Nevertheless, there they were, the opposite of right side up, suspended in the uncanny calm that comes after metal collides with rock and comes to a stop.

Like so many adventures, Thomas and Chiara's began with a map. They don't remember where they acquired it, but they do remember that their trip started to become real the moment they hung it in the kitchen of their small, Parisian apartment.

Little by little they plotted places they wanted to visit—the dunes in Merzouga, the Mauritanian coast, the volcanoes in the Andes. They took turns adding to the map, usually after a long day in the lab. A circle for yes, dashes for routes and possible detours, red hatching to mark areas to avoid. Initially, it was a way to stave off the monotony of their Ph.D.s, but with each new scribble, the dream of traveling the world for a year after finishing graduate school transformed into something tangible.

They were dedicated to their neuroscience research. Chiara studied how our brain makes trade-offs between expected effort and expected rewards. Thomas investigated the ways our brain senses our environment while we sleep. But as their Ph.D.s wore on, the hours spent isolated in the lab crowded out those spent meeting new people or seeing new places. After half a decade devoted to humans in the form of data points, they could feel their adventurous sides atrophying.

The irony for Chiara and Thomas was that even as they studied aspects of human life so deeply, they so rarely got to live it. Their curiosity to understand people and the world had led them to study the brain and behavior. But out of necessity, their curiosity had gone into hibernation. Now, little by little, it yawned, stretched, stepped back into the world. Imagining where they would go—what they would see, eat, try— became a way to feed it and experiment with an alternative reality, one free from the dictates and deadlines of their doctorates.

"There will be no trip!" Chiara's father yelled as he pounded the table. A family dinner had soured. "It's too dangerous!" This was not going well, Chiara thought. But it wasn't going unexpectedly either.

Chiara and Thomas had decided they needed to commit. They had been talking about the trip for so long, half joking, half serious, each wondering if the other would eventually nix the whole thing, whether because of a job offer or cold feet about living out of a car for a year. An unspoken game of chicken.

But neither blinked. Instead, they decided to tell people about their plans—their family, friends, and graduate school advisors. They weren't sure what everyone would think of them trading the lab for the road for a year, *at least* a year (in some versions of their imagined futures, they stayed on the road forever or wound up as shepherds in New Zealand), but they knew committing would make it harder to back out.

They would travel the world overland in the off-road Land Rover Chiara shared with her sister, the car Chiara learned to drive on when she was 17, when she had christened it Bechamel. They would outfit Bechamel with a rooftop tent and supplies that would allow them to stick to back roads. They would prepare gear for every type of weather, from below 0° F to over 100° F, versatility they would need for traveling from the Sahara to the Andes. They would sleep anywhere they wanted. They would linger or move on as they pleased.

Their advisors gave their blessing, albeit with a dose of don't-say-I-didn't-warn-you career advice. Their friends wondered if they planned to blog about their travels and seemed confused when Thomas and Chiara explained they had no instrumental motives in mind. Thomas's parents were thrilled and planned to meet them somewhere along the way. Chiara's family was less enthusiastic.

"Basta! Enough!" Chiara's father argued passionately against the trip, complete with the scowl he made when he was arguing with one of his kids, his particular way of pacing back and forth when he was upset. He was worried that, as foreigners, they would be easy targets for crime or violence. Thomas and Chiara had it in their heads to go so far, for so long, in such remote places, what would they do if something happened? What would *he* do if something happened? He tested them with barbs like, "You're like me as a child, setting up toy soldiers for battle but never actually fighting the war. You'll prepare, but you won't actually go." He even threatened to sabotage Bechamel to keep them in Europe.

Chiara spent hours reasoning with him, explaining how his perception of what might go wrong was skewed. We hear about all the trips that go horribly wrong but not the ones that go right. Statistically speaking, she told him, the thing to fear the most would be a car accident.

"**D**id you hit a llama?"

Seeing Bechamel flipped on her roof and a pair of shaky foreigners 20 yards away, two local guys pulled over to check if Thomas and Chiara were alright. Thomas, surprised by the question, explained that their two-ton vehicle had *not* run into a llama.

"Did you fall asleep?"

No. Thomas was sure he had been awake. He had been aware of what he was thinking before he crashed, so how could he be asleep? He explained that his mind was just sort of elsewhere, that he'd gotten distracted and oversteered; it was the first curve in miles.

Sizing up the damage—physical for Bechamel and psychological for Thomas and Chiara, who were shaken but uninjured—the two guys offered to help flip Bechamel back over and tow them the rest of the way to town. Thomas, still in shock, rode shotgun in the windshieldless Bechamel as one of the guys steered, the two of them eating crushed glass and road debris for

Bechamel, the 2006 Land Rover Defender. Thomas and Chiara's transport and home for a year between 2016 and 2017.

ORIGINAL PHOTO: Chiara Varazzani and Thomas Andrillon.

the half hour to Gobernador Gregores. Chiara rode in the lead vehicle, which dropped the three of them, Thomas, Chiara, and Bechamel, off at the town's only hotel.

On the road, it was easy to let your mind wander. At times, there's wasn't much else to do. And that was the point.

When they left from Chiara's parents' house in Tuscany in August 2016, the plan was to have no plan. They had a general direction in mind, but there was no itinerary. What Thomas and Chiara craved was freedom and unpredictability, serendipity and spontaneity, something other than a straight line.

Their first month on the road, they made their way from Italy through the Alps, into southern France, across the Pyrenees into Spain, south along Portugal's western coast, and then back into southern Spain. There, they crossed the Strait of Gibraltar into Morocco. For the next three months, they drove south down Africa's western edge, across the Sahara Desert and along the Atlantic. Shortly before Christmas in 2016, they boarded a freighter in Dakar, Senegal, that took them all the way to Montevideo, Uruguay, where they began their trek through South America.

With each mile that ticked by, each campsite, each sunrise and sunset, each conversation or meal shared with a stranger, they shed the expectations, habits, and routines built for the confines of their lives in Paris.

They formed new rituals. Each afternoon, they would decide where to camp for the night. They searched for places where they might be in nature, secluded, and they tried to set up in time to enjoy the sunset. They were guided by

Thomas and Chiara wandered through three continents during their year on the road.

ORIGINAL PHOTO:
Chiara Varazzani and Thomas Andrillon.

strangers they met. They followed recommendations to stop at this place or that, find someone in the next town. They trusted invitations to stay in the homes of people who, like Thomas and Chiara, were simply curious to learn about someone else's life, if for only a moment.

They tuned into their mental rhythms. In the mornings, Thomas discovered that he needed time to process his thoughts, almost as a way to finish his dreams from the night before. After driving, they learned to let their minds go free, a way to decompress after focusing on the road. They observed their power to incubate a new idea. With no pressure to bring it from the mental to the physical world until it was ready, they followed along as ideas sprang up and developed, disappeared or stuck around.

They had spent the last five years studying other people's brains. Now, the long miles on the road, outside of the lab, afforded them an intimate experience with their own.

On family trips, Thomas's dad had a rule: vacations were expensive and complicated to plan, so Thomas and his brother were not allowed to read in the car. They were expected to look out the window, to see and experience the place they traveled to. On those trips, he first experienced where the mind could take you, how wandering in the physical world paralleled wandering in the mental world.

With each mile he and Chiara wandered, Thomas became more and more curious about the activity streaming through our waking minds. In graduate school, Thomas studied sleep as a way to explore consciousness—to parse its flow and ebb, when we're awake, as we fall asleep, enter different sleep stages, and dream.

Thomas entered a field where sleep was often presented as an all or nothing phenomenon—when we're asleep we're unconscious or dreaming and, as a result, disconnected from our physical environments. But we don't fall off the bed when we sleep. Sleepwalkers avoid physical obstacles in their environment. When sleeping mothers hear the cries of their own children, they're more likely to wake than for those from other children.

For his dissertation, he investigated what happens in the brain that allows us to perceive something in our environment while we're sleeping. He conducted a series of studies to parse how the brain processes different stimuli during sleep. He found the brain could recognize language, learn patterns, determine categories, and prepare reactions, despite the brains' owners being asleep and unaware. Certain brain areas would respond with an activity similar to what they showed when awake, despite other regions showing a state of sleep. The sleeping brain isn't completely shut off from its environment.

The morning after the crash, Thomas and Chiara hustled around the town of 7,000, looking for someone who could repair Bechamel. In a bitter twist, the worst damage had occurred when the two guys right-sided Bechamel; at one point, all the weight had rested on the corner of the front, passenger-side roof, which crumpled like a crushed Coke can.

As they searched for a repair shop, they faced a repeated line of questioning. *Did they hit an animal?* No. *Asleep?* No. *Alcohol?* No. *What happened?* Distracted. *Really? That road is good.* To the locals, it didn't make sense—a crash with no cause. Eventually, after running through this script a handful of times, Thomas and Chiara gave in. They went with the llama.

Fortunately, the locals were as helpful as they were skeptical. They pointed Thomas and Chiara to a metal shop, run by a guy called El Gringo. In a few days, he estimated that he would be able to get it drivable, but he couldn't fully repair it. They would have to take it to a mechanic who had the proper tools and parts for Bechamel's aluminum body.

It wasn't ideal, but they were relieved. Their relief was brief. Chiara got news that her grandmother had passed away, and she was needed at home. She'd have to leave and meet up with Thomas later. Unable to drive their own car, she left Thomas at El Gringo's shop and hitchhiked to the nearest airport in Rio Gallegos, some 350 miles away.

So, Thomas was alone. He spent the next few days waiting for Bechamel to be patched up, then he set off on a 1,700 mile, 10-day solo drive north to Mendoza, Argentina, where there was a mechanic who could do the full repair. For two weeks he replayed the crash in his head. Why had he flipped Bechamel? What had happened

in his mind that nearly killed them? Hitting a hypothetical llama worked to satisfy people's curiosity in conversation, but it did nothing to placate his own.

"The participants look tired," Thomas's research assistant told him in 2017. "Even if they say they're mind wandering, it looks like they want to fall asleep."

That didn't seem right to Thomas. That hadn't been his experience during the trip. His hypothesis was that mind wandering was a form of impulsivity, a sign of a vivid imagination or a symptom an overactive mind, not one on the brink of sleep.

After their year on the road, Thomas and Chiara moved to Australia. Chiara was recruited to help lead the government's new behavioral science team. Thomas made good on his interest in mind wandering and landed a postdoc where he could study it.

Now, his mind-wandering research had hit upon an unexpected question. Why would people who report that their mind is wandering look like they're falling asleep?

Thomas knew there was a link between sleep and hyperactivity: people who are sleep-deprived often show sluggishness, but paradoxically, sleep deprivation causes impulsivity too. Other work showed different parts of the brain enter sleep at different times, meaning some parts are asleep while others are still awake, a sign that sleep isn't global, it's local—brain regions can enter or exit sleep and wakefulness differently. And of course, he had spent his Ph.D. figuring out how particular parts of the brain tune into our environments when we are asleep. As the pieces came together, he was surprised he was just now seeing the picture.

He set up several experiments recording participants' brain activity as they completed long and monotonous tasks. When participants reported mind wandering, Thomas found they had sleep-like waves in their prefrontal cortex— the part of the brain responsible for executive function—despite being behaviorally awake. And when their minds wandered, they were more likely to respond impulsively on the task. The wandering brain can be an impulsive brain, not because of hyperactivity or hyperarousal, as Thomas originally thought, but because sleep can creep into the waking brain.

Bechamel peers across a desert in Peru.

ORIGINAL PHOTO:
Chiara Varazzani and Thomas Andrillon.

As he drove to Mendoza alone, Thomas thought back to the day of the crash. The morning had been a particularly pleasant one. The weather was better than it had been for the past month. It wasn't as cold or windy. He and Chiara had lingered outside, tinkering with their gear and Bechamel. They found a minor electrical issue with the brake lights that they decided they wanted to get fixed. They didn't typically stay in cities, but they settled on passing through Gobernador Gregores to see if someone there could repair it.

The first road had been a road in a looser sense of the term, rough and rock covered. To avoid too much vibration, he had driven at higher speeds, gliding over the rugged surface, on high alert for larger rocks, which would damage the car. When they made it to National Route 40, Chiara had asked if him if he wanted to switch. He remembered saying he'd keep going.

Chiara had read from an almanac her father had given them for their trip. They had developed a routine of reading from it to help pass the time. Whoever the passenger was would thumb through the book, select a country, and read out loud. There was information about topography and demographics, crops, livestock, manufacturing.

She had been reading something about Myanmar. He didn't remember what, but his mind had gone to border crossings and Bechamel. Crossing the border as a person was straightforward. Crossing with a car conjured a different level of bureaucratic red tape. Governments worked hard to prevent the illegal import of cars like Bechamel. There were more regulations to study, more paperwork to fill out, and more uncertainty to navigate. What would crossing the border be like in Myanmar? Where would be the best place to cross? How long would it take to clear immigration?

Lost in his thoughts, he had noticed the curve too late. He tried to correct it but oversteered. Bechamel swerved right, then left, right, then left. He remembered cursing the laws of physics. As Bechamel began to flip down a slope, his mind had gone to his sailing days—*l'enfournage*, when a boat flips nose first. Once, he had dropped from first to last in a race this way. Then, they capsized in the Patagonian Desert.

He remembered all that. His mind had been wandering. "How could he have been asleep?" he wondered.

———

Five years after their trip, Thomas and Chiara have found their way back to Paris. There, Chiara is the lead behavioral scientist at the Organisation for Economic Co-operation and Development, helping bring together and develop government behavioral science teams from around the world. Thomas is a researcher at the Paris Brain Institute. They still have a sense of adventure, though it's taken the form of chasing their toddler, Bianca, around their apartment.

During their trip, somewhere in the Andes, Chiara remembers reading Thomas a line from *The Undoing Project*. A quote from psychologist Amos Tversky: "The secret to doing good research is always to be a little underemployed. You waste years by not being able to waste hours."

For Thomas, the discovery that sleep intrudes our waking lives when we're mind wandering means that the borders we've used to define our mental lives are more porous than we think. We spend about one-third of our lives asleep, and 50 percent of our waking hours mind wandering. What it means to be asleep or awake, conscious or unconscious, dreaming or not, may be less distinct, more continuous, full of grays and in-betweens, liminal spaces he's just beginning to explore.

Traveling the world by car might not be the fastest way to get somewhere, but isn't that the point? When we wander physically or mentally, what shapes us is the process. We create new connections and rid ourselves of old ones. Borders blur and we venture off path. We find ourselves in places unexpected. ■

———

Evan Nesterak is the editor of Behavioral Scientist.

The Kahneman-Treisman Center for Behavioral Science & Public Policy, housed in Princeton University's School of Public and International Affairs, leverages the combined strengths of the University's faculty across a range of disciplines. The Center's affiliates identify new approaches to address social challenges and improve lives. It is the intellectual hub that supports and organizes new research projects, plans lecture series and conferences, disseminates research results, and connects Princeton researchers and students with policymakers and scholars from other institutions.

Find out more at **behavioralpolicy.princeton.edu**

PART 3

Journey to Robbers Cave

THE GENERAL DESIGN of all three camps was roughly the same: first, the boys were divided into two groups. In the first two camps, these groups were selected after the boys had formed friendships in order to purposefully split up friend groups, whereas in the third camp, the groups were preselected and the boys were initially unaware there was another group of campers. Through a series of team building activities—hikes, cookouts, overnight campouts, swimming— the groups bonded, spontaneously formed their own leadership structures, and created their own group culture.

The research team tried to stoke the rivalry between the two groups through a series of tournament style events, including baseball, tug-of-war, touch football, tent pitching, skits, songs, and cabin inspection; pocket knives were offered as prizes for the tournament winners.

The tournament succeeded in creating friction between the groups, friction which increased as the contest progressed. The boys began to trade taunts and insults; they also planned raids on the opposing cabin, turning over bunks and dumping personal possessions on the floor. In 1954, the Eagles stole and burned the flag of their rivals, the Rattlers; in retaliation the Rattlers stole a pair of jeans from the Eagles' appointed leader and painted them with the words "The Last of the Eagles" in bright orange paint and then carried the jeans as a flag.

With animosity and overt aggression growing between the groups, the researchers turned their focus to the core of the experiment: bringing the groups back into a state of harmony. Sherif believed that resolving the conflict at the camps would provide valuable insight into the social and psychological process for how to secure peace between warring nations. The success of his vision hinged on this final stage—but resolving conflict would prove difficult to achieve.

CALENDAR OF *STAGES* ~~EVENTS~~

Happy Valley Camp

	Day No.		
STAGE I, Spontaneous Groupings	1	Mon. Aug 15	
	2	Tues. " 16	
	3	Wed. " 17	First sociograms
STAGE II, In-Group Formation (Intra-Group Relations)	1	Thur. " 18	Hike and cookout
	2	Fri. " 19	*Strengthening of in-groups setting boundaries and raids.*
	3	Sat. " 20	Bulldogs' overnight campout
	4	Sun. " 21	Red Devils' overnight campout
	5	Mon. " 22	Second sociograms
STAGE III, Inter-Group Relations (Effects on Intra-Group Relations)	1	Tues. " 23	Softball game
	2	Wed. " 24	Soccer game
	3	Thur. " 25	Football, end of contest, party fr... t...
	4	Fri. " 26	Lunch frustration, end of Stage III in the afternoon
Immediate Aftermath of Stage III		Sat. " 27	Attempted raids by Red Devils
STAGE IV, In-Group Disintegration		Sun. " 28	
		Mon. " 29	
		Tues. " 30	
		Wed. " 31	
		Thur Sept 1	
		Fri. " 2	

A calendar of camp events organized by the experimental stages at the 1949 camp.

S. No.	Ht.	Wt.	Sports	Special Sports	Popularity	Other Skills	Swim	Camp Experience	Remarks	Group
1 B	4-9½	77	g	Ball	+	sing cook	o	o		B
2 B	5-3	115	"g"	Ball Pitcher	+	art + sing	x	Day camp		B
3 B	4-7	72	"g"	OA	+	art + sing skits	o	o		B
4 A	4-9	97	g. high int.	ball football	+	cook skits art	+	x		A

A handwritten chart listing data about each camper—including height, weight, popularity, sports, and skills—as part of the process to divide campers into two matched groups.

Photographs of the boys engaged in standard summer camp activities: archery, canoeing, swimming, setting up tents.

JOURNEY TO ROBBERS CAVE Part 3

Segment of edited presentation notes in which Sherif describes the growing antagonism between the campers and the attempts by one group to "raid" the cabin of the other group.

In spite of genuine efforts of the participant observers and junior counsellors to stop these physical manifestations of group antagonism, the acts and words of hostility continued in the days that followed. One of the most crucial of the manifestations of hostility during this period was an attempted 2 A.M. raid *planned* by the Red Devils which they tried to keep secrete from their participant observer and junior counsellor. In spite of the fact that they were dead tired from the activities of the day, the boys succeeded in awakening and dressing at 2 A.M. one morning. The raid was stopped by the participant observer when one of the would-be raiders kicked over a barrel of green apples which had been collected as ammunition, thus waking the participant observer and his assistant who were *asleep* ~~asleep~~ in the cabin. Pictures were made of the boys collecting these apples and of the hoarded ammunition which ~~they were~~ *was* later ~~made to dump~~ *dumped.*

(Pictures) (Slides 18, 19, 20, 21)

A tournament of competitive events was used to build conflict between the groups, including popular activities like tug-of-war.

In 1954, the Eagles stole the flag of the Rattlers and burned a portion of it to taunt the other campers; in retaliation the Rattlers stole the jeans of one of the Eagles and transformed them into a flag with a painted threat: "Last of the Eagles."

Vaccinating in

In June 2012, North Waziristan's Taliban leader issued a fatwa banning polio vaccination campaigns. Other Pakistani Taliban leaders in Khyber Pakhtunkhwa and South Waziristan quickly followed suit. Pamphlets dispersed throughout these regions made it known that anyone involved in the vaccination campaign moving forward would be subject to great loss and harm.

That harm came swiftly.

In Karachi, a doctor working for the polio program was shot while traveling through a resistant part of the city. One by one, polio vaccinators—predominantly women working for just a few dollars a day—were being targeted and killed. Police officers assigned to protect them would soon meet the same fate. By 2015, an estimated 70 polio vaccine workers had been assassinated.

It wasn't because the Taliban was against vaccination. In fact, militant groups in Pakistan and Afghanistan had been facilitating access and guaranteeing vaccine coverage in their territories for years. But in these particular conflict-affected areas, polio eradication was a powerful leverage point. The communities stifling polio campaigns backed by the United States and Western nations were the same communities being brought to their knees by U.S. drone strikes. In this political minefield, anti-Western narratives easily took root. The Taliban's 2012 directive was firm: stop the drone strikes and we'll allow vaccination.

The unexpected recipient of that message was the Global Polio Eradication Initiative, the only public health program that sends vaccinators door-to-door in remote, underserved communities throughout the world. They aim to reach every child under-five with polio drops, multiple times, until virus transmission is interrupted.

Equipped with vaccine coolers, vaccination teams set off in the earliest hours of the morning. They often walk for miles to reach communities left behind by health systems and basic infrastructure. Outside of every home they visit, they leave a small mark. Sometimes these markings look like fractions, denoting the number of children vaccinated out of the total number of children living there. Other times they are big X's, signifying a household that refused the vaccine altogether. In areas that lack centralized and accurate data on their residents, these symbols scrawled across doorways, gates, and makeshift entryways ensure that every child is counted and, ideally, protected.

For nearly a decade, we worked as behavior change specialists for UNICEF's polio eradication team, one of the core member-organizations of the Global Polio Eradication Initiative. We were just two out of hundreds of national and international civil servants, alongside tens of thousands of frontline workers striving toward the same, singular objective—eliminate polio from the Earth, so that no child has to suffer from a lifetime of preventable paralysis. In the 1980s and 90s, polio was paralyzing over 350,000 kids each year. Because of efforts like this one, by 2011 that number was down to several hundred cases a year.

The global strategy to build demand for the polio vaccine was to increase knowledge and awareness of the dangers of polio among parents with young children. Before each campaign, radio and TV spots would air, and thousands of health workers and community

Taliban Country

By Sherine Guirguis and Michael Coleman

mobilizers would take to the streets, often with megaphones in hand, to announce campaign dates and to remind parents to make sure that their children were home when the vaccinators came knocking. By 2011, that approach had successfully eradicated wild poliovirus in all but three countries in the world: Nigeria, Afghanistan, and Pakistan.

In northern Nigeria and other countries, there had been incidents of rock throwing, knife wielding, and even cases of vaccinators getting kidnapped by aggressive resistors to the vaccine. It was not uncommon for communities to furnish a list of demands in exchange for vaccinating their children. These would often include paved roads or reliable electricity: things that were vital, if difficult, to deliver. The program was no stranger to resistance, but the violence erupting in Pakistan was unlike anything the public health world had ever witnessed.

At first, we saw the bans in the same way we saw the rocks, blades, and lists brandished at vaccinators: reckless, instead of relatable. *How could they use their children as a bargaining chip? How could they not want to protect their children?*

We began to realize that we were asking the wrong questions.

Behind the polio bans were some of the poorest, most marginalized communities in the world. Like all parents, they wanted the best for their kids. For us, that meant vaccines. For them, it meant safe roads, school buildings, and health clinics. It meant clear and harmless skies. Doorways free of fractions that might turn their homes into targets. Taliban leaders may not have been fully representing community views, but everyone was trying to protect their children

in the way that made the most sense for their context—a context we didn't fully understand.

Complicating matters further was the recent news that the CIA used a door-to-door vaccine campaign in 2011 to confirm Osama bin Laden's whereabouts. Their fraudulent campaign was for hepatitis B, but it didn't matter. The process was stained. The national polio eradication effort, known by every Pakistani as the dose brought to your door, was now inextricably linked to U.S. surveillance.

The violence in Pakistan was our first encounter with the notion that the Global Polio Eradication Initiative's singular approach to disease eradication could fail or, worse, do harm. The model that relied on a consistent supply of vaccines conveniently delivered to households was not fit for purpose in these conflict-affected, deeply polarized communities. This epidemiological approach didn't sufficiently consider the cultural, social, and political webs that these children and their parents were tangled within.

Until this point, our role had been to design strategies to motivate parents to vaccinate their children, not militant leaders taking the reins of underserved, war-torn communities. We felt monumentally ill-equipped to design behavioral strategies that could motivate the Taliban, or the communities they represented, to welcome vaccination given all that it represented. Suddenly, the long-established model felt too small. Yet we felt we had to do something. Every month under the Taliban's decree left 200,000 children under the age of five unvaccinated.

We decided to break the model wide open. We got in touch with people who could offer a view from the outside of the program. We phoned political scientists and writers, behavioral researchers and pollsters, social marketers, security experts, filmmakers, musicians, and artists. We sought the people who understood the heartbeat of Pakistan, the patterns of the Taliban, and the ways of Pashtun tribes. We gathered those fluent in the dynamics of conflict, politics, and negotiation.

We brought these individuals together with our Pakistani colleagues in a Dutch conference room off the North Sea. We wanted everyone to use the neutral ground to share their distinct perspectives. With the help of these fresh eyes, we could see the harm of sending unfamiliar vaccinators into the homes of families who had become much too familiar with danger and its countless shapes. We could recognize the irony of a free health service delivered by foreign and domestic governments who filled their skies with smoke and left their streets abandoned. By the end of the week, people who had never thought about polio eradication were working alongside those who had dedicated their lives to it, cocreating solutions to a crisis that had long been mistaken as purely biomedical.

If we wanted a chance at restoring the vaccination campaign and eliminating polio, the program would need to change its face. There needed to be a public handoff to local Pakistani, Islamic, and Pashtun leaders. Vaccine coolers reading *END POLIO NOW* in English would need to be revised, recolored, and delivered in Urdu or, ideally, Pashto. The call to vaccinate needed to come more publicly from Muslim and Pashtun organizations and individuals that people could trust. The program would need to engage with communities to ensure that vaccination, and health care in general, was respectfully delivered and presented to meet their needs, not ours.

These ideas didn't change the program overnight. It would take much more than a conference room full of hopefuls to change a 25-year-old global eradication effort. But these discussions planted seeds of possibility among us and others in the program. It was clear that public health could and should be collaborative, interdisciplinary, creative, and designed for those at the center of it. We left our jobs and founded Common Thread to focus full-time on building a new approach to public health guided by these principles.

In our work today, we try to ask the questions we didn't know to ask back in 2012. How can we incorporate local culture, social norms, and politics into every public health strategy? How can the lived experiences of those we aim to serve change the way we design health services? How do we create solutions that respond to the needs, desires, and behavior of people living under pressures we can never fully comprehend? How do we cater to the beliefs of the resistant and those with radically opposite views?

We now know that to disparage those who oppose public health measures only deepens the divide. We now know, too, that to understand the fabric of communities is just as important as biomedical science to design equitable and effective public health policies. But most of all, we know that these lessons, and these questions, are only the beginning—and that by seeking to understand communities and honor their priorities as our own, we can find a path to better health for everyone. ∎

Sherine Guirguis is a founder, director, and lead strategist at Common Thread. She's been creating powerful narratives with data for over 20 years. She's held senior behavior change positions at UNICEF, leading large-scale behavior change strategies in response to the Indian Ocean tsunami, West Africa's Ebola outbreak, and polio eradication. Sherine holds a M.Sc. in public health from the London School of Hygiene and Tropical Medicine, and an M.A. in international relations and economics from Johns Hopkins University.

Michael Coleman is a founder, director, and lead storyteller at Common Thread. He's held senior communications posts with UN agencies in Angola, Pakistan, and Vietnam and has an extensive background in social development, documentary production, and journalism through work in Honduras, Sri Lanka, Canada and Poland. Michael holds an M.A. in political communications from Goldsmiths, University of London.

THE
BEHAVIORAL
INSIGHTS
TEAM

A deep understanding of human behavior is key to creating a world where people and communities can thrive.

The Behavioral Insights Team (BIT) is working towards this future. We are a global social-purpose consultancy that uses behavioral science research to design more equitable policies and systems. Created in the U.K. government as the first "nudge unit" in 2010, we now have more than 200 staff, and offices in seven countries worldwide. Our teams partner with governments, nonprofits, and the private sector to reach their goals across a wide range of policy areas—from health and the environment to education and the economy.

Visit **bi.team** to learn more

CHAPTER 4

Discoveries

"[Discovery] consists of seeing what everybody has seen and thinking what nobody has thought."

—ALBERT SZENT-GYÖRGYI
BY WAY OF ARTHUR SCHOPENHAUER

Unraveling the Myth of Universal Emotions

By Lisa Feldman Barrett

According to the classical view of emotion, our faces hold the key to assessing emotions objectively and accurately. A primary inspiration for this idea is Charles Darwin's book *The Expression of the Emotions in Man and Animals,* where he claimed that emotions and their expressions were an ancient part of universal human nature. All people, everywhere in the world, are said to exhibit and recognize facial expressions of emotion without any training whatsoever.

The human face is laced with 42 small muscles on each side. The facial movements that we see each other make every day—winks and blinks, smirks and grimaces, raised and wrinkled brows—occur when combinations of facial muscles contract and relax, causing connective tissue and skin to move. Even when your face seems completely still to the naked eye, your muscles are still contracting and relaxing.

According to the classical view, each emotion is displayed on the face as a particular pattern of movements—a "facial expression." When you're happy, you're supposed to smile. When you're angry, you're supposed to furrow your brow. These movements are said to be part of the "fingerprint" of their respective emotions.

Back in the 1960s, the psychologist Silvan S. Tomkins and his protégés Carroll E. Izard and Paul Ekman decided to test this in the lab. They created sets of meticulously posed photographs, such as those in figure 1, to represent six so-called basic emotions they believed had biological fingerprints: anger, fear, disgust, surprise, happiness, and sadness. These photos, which featured actors who were carefully coached, were supposed to be the clearest examples of facial expressions for these emotions. (They might look exaggerated or artificial to you, but they were designed this way on purpose, because Tomkins believed they gave the strongest, clearest signals for emotion.)

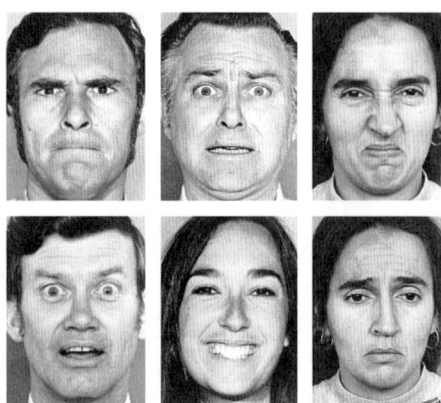

Figure 1: Some facial photographs from basic emotion method studies

Using posed photos like these, Tomkins and his crew applied an experimental technique to study how well people "recognize" emotional expressions, or, more precisely, how well they perceive facial movements as expressions of emotion. Hundreds of published experiments have used this method, and it's still considered the gold standard today. A test subject is given a photograph and a set of emotion words, as in figure 2.

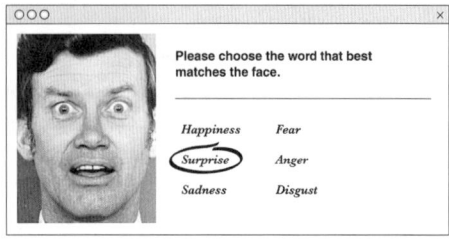

Figure 2: Basic emotion method: picking a word to match the face

The subject then chooses the word that best matches the face. In this case, the intended word is "Surprise." Or, using a slightly different setup, a test subject is given two posed photos and a brief story, as in figure 3, and then picks which face best matches the story. In this case, the intended face is on the right.

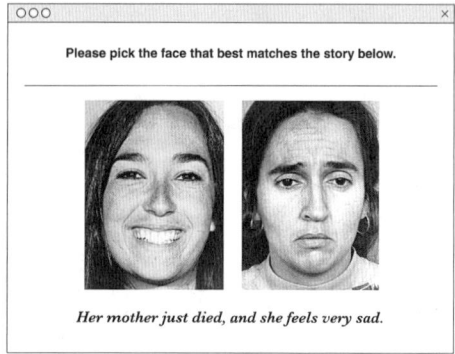

Figure 3: Basic emotion method: picking a face to match the story

This research technique—let's call it the basic emotion method—revolutionized the scientific study of what Tomkins's group called "emotion recognition." Using this method, scientists showed that people from around the world could consistently match the same emotion words (translated into the local language) to posed faces. In one famous study, Ekman and his colleagues traveled to Papua New Guinea and ran experiments with a local population, the Fore people, who had little contact with the Western world. Even this remote tribe could consistently match the faces to the expected emotion words and stories. In later years, scientists ran similar studies in many other countries such as Japan and Korea. In each case, subjects easily matched the posed scowls, pouts, smiles, and so on to the provided emotion words or stories.

From this evidence, scientists concluded that emotion recognition is universal: no matter where you are born or grow up, you should be able to recognize American-style facial expressions like those in the photos. The only way expressions could be universally recognized, the reasoning went, is if they are universally produced: thus, facial expressions must be reliable, diagnostic fingerprints of emotion.

Other scientists, however, worried that the basic emotion method was too indirect and subjective to reveal emotion fingerprints because it involves human judgment. A more objective technique, called facial electromyography (EMG), removes human perceivers altogether. Facial EMG places electrodes on the surface of the skin to detect the electrical signals that make facial muscles move. It precisely identifies the parts of the face as they move, how much, and how often. As it turns out, facial EMG presents a serious challenge to the classical view of emotion. In study after study, the muscle movements do not reliably indicate when someone is angry, sad, or fearful; they don't form predictable fingerprints for each emotion. At best, facial EMG reveals that these movements distinguish pleasant versus unpleasant feeling. Even more damning, the facial movements recorded in these studies do not reliably match the posed photos created for the basic emotion method.

Scientists also employ an alternative technique called facial action coding (FACS), in which trained observers laboriously classify a subject's individual facial movements as they occur. It's less objective than facial EMG, since it relies on human perceivers, but presumably more objective than matching words to posed faces in the basic emotion method. Nevertheless, the movements observed during facial action coding also don't consistently match the posed photos.

Other scientists have also demonstrated that we take tremendous information about emotion from the surrounding context. They graft photographs of faces and bodies that don't belong together, like an angry scowling face attached to a body that's holding a dirty diaper, and their test subjects nearly always identify the emotion appropriate to the body, not the face—in this case, disgust rather than anger. Faces are constantly moving, and your brain relies on many different factors at once—body posture, voice, the overall situation, your lifetime of experience—to figure out which movements are meaningful and what they mean.

When it comes to emotion, a face doesn't speak for itself. In fact, the poses of the basic emotion method were not discovered by observing faces in the real world. Scientists *stipulated* those facial poses, inspired by Darwin's book, and asked actors to portray them. And now these faces are simply assumed to be the universal expressions of emotion.

But they aren't universal. One way my lab and I have demonstrated this is by conducting a study using photos from a group of emotion experts—accomplished actors. The photos came from the book *In Character: Actors Acting,* in which actors portray emotions by posing their faces to match written scenarios. We divided our U.S. test subjects into three groups. The first group read only the scenarios, for example, "He just witnessed a shooting on his quiet, tree-shaded block in Brooklyn." A second group saw only the facial configurations, such as Martin Landau's pose for the shooting scenario (figure 4, center). A third group saw the scenarios and the faces. In each case, we handed subjects a short list of emotion words to categorize whatever emotion they saw.

For the shooting scenario I just mentioned, 66 percent of subjects who read the scenario alone or with Landau's face rated the scenario as a fearful situation. But for subjects who saw Landau's face alone, devoid of context, only 38 percent of them rated it as fear and 56 percent rated it as surprise. (Figure 4 compares Landau's facial configuration to basic emotion method photos for "fear" and "surprise." Does Landau look afraid or surprised? Or both?)

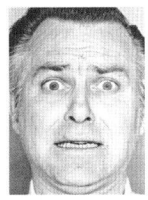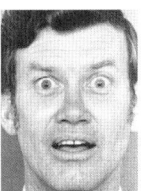

Figure 4: Actor Martin Landau (center) flanked by basic emotion method faces for fear (left) and surprise (right)

Other actors' poses for fear were strikingly different from Landau's. In one case, the actress Melissa Leo portrayed fear for the scenario: "She is trying to decide if she should tell her husband about a rumor going around that she is gay before he hears it from someone else." Her mouth is closed and downturned, and her brow is slightly knitted. Nearly three-quarters of our test subjects who saw her face alone rated it as sad, but when presented with the scenario, 70 percent of subjects rated her face as displaying fear. This sort of variation held true for every emotion that we studied. An emotion like "Fear" does not have a single expression but a *diverse population of facial movements* that vary from one situation to the next. (Think about it: When is the last time an actor won an Academy Award for pouting when sad?)

This may seem obvious once you pause to consider your own emotional experiences. When you experience an emotion such as fear, you might move your face in a variety of ways. While cowering in your seat at a horror movie, you might close your eyes or cover them with your hands. If you're uncertain whether a person directly in front of you could harm you, you might narrow your eyes to see the person's face better. If danger is potentially lurking around the next corner, your eyes might widen to improve your peripheral vision. "Fear" takes no single physical form. Variation is the norm. Likewise, happiness, sadness, anger, and every other emotion you know is a diverse *category*, with widely varying facial movements.

If facial movements have so much variation within an emotion category like "Fear," you might wonder why we find it so natural to believe that a wide-eyed face is the universal fear expression. The answer is that it's a stereotype, a symbol that fits a well-known theme for "Fear" within our culture. Preschools teach these stereotypes to children: "People who scowl are angry. People who pout are sad." They are cultural shorthands or conventions. You see them in cartoons, in advertisements, in the faces of dolls, in emojis—in an endless array of imagery and iconography. Textbooks teach these stereotypes to psychology students. Therapists teach them to their patients. The media spreads them widely throughout the Western world. "Now, wait just a minute," you might be thinking. "Is she saying that our culture has *created* these expressions, and we all have *learned* them?" Well . . . yes. And the classical view perpetuates these stereotypes as if they are authentic fingerprints of emotion.

To be sure, faces are instruments of social communication. Some facial movements have meaning, but others do not, and right now, we know precious little about how people figure out which is which, other than that context is somehow crucial (body language, social situation, cultural expectation, etc.). When facial movements do convey a psychological message—say, raising an eyebrow—we don't know if the message is always emotional, or even if its meaning is the same each time. If we put all the scientific evidence together, we cannot claim, with any reasonable certainty, that each emotion has a diagnostic facial expression.

Universal laws have an annoying habit of losing their universality. Newton's law of universal gravitation was only universal until the theory of relativity showed that it wasn't.

With this in mind, watch what happens to so-called universal facial expressions when we change the basic emotion method very slightly. Simply remove the list of emotion words. Test subjects must now *freely label* the same posed photographs from the dozens (or even hundreds) of emotion words that they know, as depicted in figure 5, instead of choosing a response from a short list of possibilities, as depicted in figure 2. When we do this, the subjects' success rate plummets. In one of the first free labeling studies ever conducted, subjects named the faces with the expected emotion words (or synonyms) only 58 percent of the time, and in subsequent studies the results were even lower. In fact, if you ask a more neutral question without referring to emotion at all—"What word best describes what's going on inside this person?"—the performance is even worse.

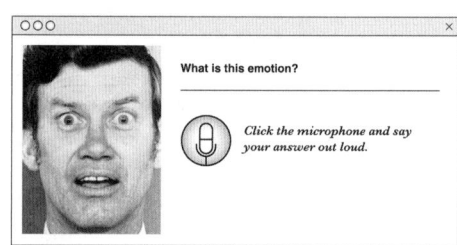

Figure 5: Basic emotion method with the emotion words removed

Why does such a small change make such a large difference? Because the short list of emotion words in the basic emotion method—a technique called a *forced choice*—is an unintentional cheat sheet for the test subjects. The words not only limit the available choices but also prompt the subjects' brains to recall facial configurations for the corresponding emotion concepts, preparing them to see certain emotions and not others. This process is called *priming*. Test subjects who see a list of emotion words are primed with the corresponding emotion concepts to categorize the posed faces they see. Your knowledge of concepts is a key ingredient for experiencing other people as emotional, and emotion words invoke this ingredient. And they could be largely responsible for producing what looks like universal emotion perception in the hundreds of studies that use the basic emotion method.

Free labeling reduced the ingredient of concept knowledge, but only somewhat. In my own lab, we went a step further and removed all emotion words, printed or spoken. On each trial of an experiment, we presented subjects with two *wordless* photographs side by side (figure 6) and asked, "Do these people feel the same emotion?" The expected answer was merely yes or no. The results of this face-matching task were telling: subjects identified the expected matches only 42 percent of the time.

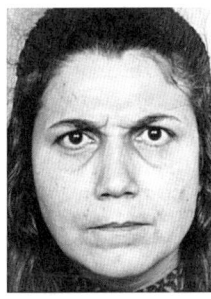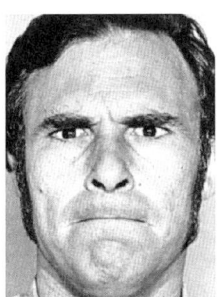

Figure 6: Basic emotion method with no words at all. Do these faces show the same emotion?

Next, our team reduced the ingredients even further. We actively interfered with our test subjects' access to their own emotion concepts, using a simple experimental technique. We had them repeat an emotion word like "anger" over and over. Eventually, the word becomes just a sound to the subject ("ang-gurr") that's mentally disconnected from its meaning. This technique has the same effect as creating a temporary brain lesion, but it's completely safe and lasts less than one second. Then we immediately showed subjects two wordless faces side by side as before. Their performance dropped to a dismal 36 percent: nearly *two-thirds* of their yes/no decisions were incorrect!

We also tested subjects with permanent brain lesions who suffer from a neurodegenerative illness called semantic dementia. These patients have trouble remembering words and concepts, including those for emotion. We gave them thirty-six photographs: six actors each posing six different basic emotion facial configurations (smiles depicting happiness, pouts depicting sadness, scowls depicting anger, wide-eyed gasping depicting fear, nose-wrinkling depicting disgust, and neutral). The patients then sorted the photos into piles in any way that was meaningful to them. They were unable to group all scowling faces into an anger pile, all pouting faces into a sadness pile, and so on. Instead, the patients produced only positive, negative, and neutral piles, an arrangement that merely reflects pleasant versus unpleasant feeling. We now had solid evidence that emotion concepts are necessary for seeing emotion in faces.

Our findings are reinforced by research on young children and infants, whose emotion concepts aren't fully developed yet. A series of experiments by psychologists James A. Russell and Sherri C. Widen showed that two- and three-year-old children, when shown basic emotion facial configurations, are not able to freely label them until they possess clearly differentiated concepts for "anger," "sadness," "fear," and so on. Such young children use words like "sad," "mad," and "scared" interchangeably. It's not an issue of understanding the emotion words; even when these kids learn the meanings, they struggle to match up two pouting faces, whereas they find it easy to match a pouting face to the word "sad." Results for infants are similarly telling. Infants who are four to eight months old, for example, can distinguish smiling faces from scowling faces. This ability, however, turned out not to be related to emotion per se. In those experiments, the posed faces for happiness showed teeth while those for anger did not, and that's the cue that infants picked up on.

From this sequence of experiments—removing the list of emotion words, then using wordless photographs, then temporarily disabling emotion concepts, then testing lesion patients who can no longer process emotion concepts, and finally testing infants who don't yet possess clearly defined emotion concepts—a theme emerges. As emotion concepts become more remote, people do worse and worse at recognizing the emotions that the posed stereotypes are supposedly displaying. This progression is strong evidence that people see an emotion in a face only if they possess the corresponding emotion concept, because they require that knowledge to construct perceptions in the moment.

To really see the power of emotion concepts, my lab visited a remote culture in Africa with little or no knowledge of Western practices and norms.

With the fast pace of globalization, very few such isolated cultures exist anymore. My doctoral student Maria Gendron traveled to Namibia to study emotion perception in a tribe known as the Himba, along with the cognitive psychologist Debi Roberson.

Maria used the face-sorting experiment with the 36 posed faces. It doesn't depend on words at all, let alone emotion words, so it worked nicely across the language and culture barriers. We'd created a set of photos using dark-skinned actors, because our originals featured Western faces that didn't look like Himba tribespeople. Our Himba subjects were able to sort the faces spontaneously by actor. When asked to sort the faces by emotion, the Himba clearly diverged from Westerners. They placed all the smiling faces into a single pile, and most of the wide-eyed faces into a second pile, but then made many different piles with mixtures of the remaining faces. If emotion perception is universal, then the Himba subjects should have sorted the photographs into six piles. When we asked our Himba subjects to freely label their piles, smiling faces were not "happy" (*ohange*) but "laughing" (*ondjora*). Wide-eyed faces were not "fearful" (*okutira*) but "looking" (*tarera*). In other words, the Himba participants categorized facial movements as behaviors rather than inferring mental states or feelings. Overall, our Himba subjects showed no evidence of universal emotion perception. And since we omitted all reference to English emotion concepts in our experiments, those concepts are a prime suspect for why the basic emotion method appears to give evidence of universality.

Maria Gendron (right) working with a Himba participant in Namibia, beneath a tent attached to Maria's truck

If you look closely at the original cross-cultural experiments from the 1960s, you can see clues that the conceptual elements within the basic emotion method pushed the results toward the appearance of universality. Of the seven samples using test subjects from remote cultures, the four that used the basic emotion method provided strong evidence for universality, but the remaining three used free labeling and did not show evidence of universality. These three contrary samples were not published in peer-reviewed journals but only as book chapters—a lesser form of publishing in the world of academia—and are rarely cited. As a result, the four samples supporting universality were lauded as a major breakthrough in research on our underlying human nature and set the stage for the research avalanche to come. Hundreds of subsequent studies employed the basic emotion method with forced choice, largely in cultures that had exposure to Western cultural practices and norms, taking a key condition for universality out of the experimental design but still claiming it as fact. This explains why today, many scientists and the public fundamentally misunderstand what is known about "emotional expressions" and "emotion recognition" from a scientific point of view.

What might the science of emotion look like today had someone drawn different conclusions from those original studies? Consider Ekman's account of his first visit to the Fore tribe in New Guinea:

I asked them to make up a story about each facial expression [photograph]. "Tell me what is happening now, what happened before to make the person show this expression, and what is going to happen next." It was like pulling teeth. I am not certain whether it was the translation process, or the fact that they have no idea what it was I wanted to hear or why I wanted them to do this. Perhaps making up stories about strangers was just something the Fore didn't do.

Ekman might be right, but it is also possible that the Fore did not understand or accept the concept of a facial "expression," which implies an internal feeling that seeks release in a set of facial movements. Not all cultures understand emotions as internal mental states. Himba and Hadza emotion concepts, for example, appear to be more focused on actions. This is also true of certain Japanese emotion concepts. The Ifaluk of Micronesia consider emotions as transactions between people. To them, anger is not a feeling of rage, a scowl, a pounding fist, or a loud yelling voice, all within the skin of one person, but a situation in which two people are engaged in a script—a dance, if you will—around a common goal. In the Ifaluk view, anger does not "live" inside either participant.

When scientists set aside the classical view and just look at the data, a radically different explanation for emotion comes to light. In short, we find that your emotions are not built-in but made from more basic parts. They are not universal but vary from culture to culture. They are not triggered; you create them. They emerge as a combination of the physical properties of your body, a flexible brain that wires itself to whatever environment it develops in, and your culture and upbringing, which provide that environment. Emotions are real, but not in the objective sense that molecules or neurons are real. They are real in the same sense that money is real—that is, hardly an illusion, but a product of human agreement.

This view, which I call the theory of constructed emotion, offers a very different interpretation of emotional events. For example, I remember being devasted while listening to Dannel Malloy, then governor of Connecticut,

speak about the tragic shooting at Sandy Hook Elementary School in 2012. At one point in his speech, my stomach knotted into a ball. My eyes flooded. The TV camera panned to the crowd where other people had started to sob too. As for Governor Malloy, he stopped speaking and was gazing downward.

Emotions like Governor Malloy's and mine seem primal—hardwired into us, reflexively deployed, shared with all our fellow humans. When triggered, they seem to unleash themselves in each of us in basically the same way. My sadness was like Governor Malloy's sadness was like the crowd's sadness.

Humanity has understood sadness and other emotions in this way for over two thousand years. But at the same time, if humanity has learned anything from centuries of scientific discovery, it's that things aren't always what they appear to be.

When I listened to Governor Malloy's speech, it did not trigger a brain circuit for sadness inside me, causing a distinctive set of bodily changes. Rather, I felt sadness in that moment because, having been raised in a certain culture, I learned long ago that "sadness" is something that may occur when certain bodily feelings coincide with terrible loss. Using bits and pieces of past experience, such as my knowledge of shootings and my previous sadness about them, my brain rapidly predicted what my body should do to cope with such tragedy. Its predictions caused my thumping heart, my flushed face, and the knots in my stomach. They directed me to cry, an action that would calm my nervous system. And they made the resulting sensations meaningful as an instance of sadness.

In this manner, my brain *constructed* my experience of emotion. My particular movements and sensations were not a fingerprint for sadness. With different predictions, my skin would cool rather than flush and my stomach would remain unknotted, yet my brain could still transform the resulting sensations into sadness. Not only that, but my original thumping heart, flushed face, knotted stomach, and tears could become meaningful as a different emotion, such as anger or fear, instead of sadness. Or in a very different situation, like a wedding celebration, those same sensations could become joy or gratitude.

After Governor Malloy's speech, as I came back to myself, wiping my tears, I was reminded that no matter what I *know* about emotions as a scientist, I *experience* them much as the classical view conceives them. My sadness felt like an instantly recognizable wave of bodily changes and feelings that overwhelmed me as a reaction to tragedy and loss. If I were not a scientist using experiments to reveal that emotions are in fact made and not triggered, I too would trust my immediate experience.

The theory of constructed emotion might not fit the way you typically experience emotion and, in fact, may well violate your deepest beliefs about how the mind works, where humans come from, and why we act and feel as we do. But the theory consistently predicts and explains the scientific evidence on emotion, including plenty of evidence that the classical view struggles to make sense of.

Each time a scientific "fact" is overturned, it leads to new avenues for discovery. The physicist Albert Michelson won a Nobel Prize in 1907 for disproving a conjecture made by Aristotle, that light travels through empty space via a hypothetical substance called luminiferous ether. His detective work set the stage for Albert Einstein's theory of relativity. In our case, we've cast substantial doubt on the evidence for universal emotions. They only *appear* to be universal *under certain conditions*— when you give people a tiny bit of information about Western emotion concepts, intentionally or not. These observations, and others like them, set the stage for the new theory of emotion. So Tomkins, Ekman, and their colleagues did contribute to a remarkable discovery. It just wasn't the discovery that they expected.

The many cross-cultural studies employing the basic emotion method suggest something else exciting: it may be easy to teach emotion concepts across cultural boundaries, even unintentionally. Such a worldwide understanding would be hugely beneficial. The Gulf War in Iraq was launched, in part, because Saddam Hussein's half-brother thought he could read the emotions of the American negotiators and informed Saddam that the United States wasn't serious about attacking. If he had only understood the American emotion concept of anger, he might have perceived anger in Secretary of State James Baker, which might have averted the first Gulf War with the United States, saving thousands of lives.

The problems with the basic emotion method demonstrate how easy it is to teach emotion concepts by accident. If scientists continue using Western stereotypes of emotion in cultural research, in the long run, they are very likely helping to create the universality that they believe they are discovering.

Scientists continue to replicate my lab's findings in other cultures (data from China, East Africa, Melanesia, and other regions are looking promising at press time). As they do, we are speeding the paradigm shift to a new understanding of emotion that goes beyond Western stereotypes. We can cast aside questions like "How accurately can you recognize fear?" and instead study the variety of facial movements that people actually make in fear.

Scientific revolutions tend to emerge not from a sudden discovery but by asking better questions. How are emotions made, if they aren't simply triggered reactions? Why do they vary so much, and why have we believed for so long that they have distinctive fingerprints? These questions in and of themselves can be delightfully interesting to ponder. But taking pleasure in the unknown is more than just a scientific indulgence. It's part of the spirit of adventure that makes us human. ∎

Excerpted from How Emotions Are Made *by Lisa Barrett. Copyright © 2017 by Lisa Feldman Barrett. Reprinted by permission of Mariner Books, an imprint of HarperCollins Publishers. All rights reserved.*

Lisa Feldman Barrett is a University Distinguished Professor of Psychology at Northeastern University. She also holds appointments at Harvard Medical School and Massachusetts General Hospital, where she is chief science officer for the Center for Law, Brain & Behavior. She is the author of *How Emotions Are Made* and *Seven and a Half Lessons About the Brain.*

Character LAB

Though we know that character is important and malleable, scientific insights that tell us how to develop character in kids are scarce. There is a lack of knowledge about which insights work, for whom, and under what conditions.

Character Lab is a nonprofit organization that connects researchers with educators to create greater knowledge about the conditions that lead to social, emotional, academic, and physical well-being for young people throughout the country. Character Lab helps researchers and schools facilitate research at scale, providing an infrastructure that cuts the time of a typical research cycle in half.

To learn more, go to **characterlab.org**

PART 4

Journey to Robbers Cave

FOR SHERIF AND HIS COLLEAGUES, having the boys develop an affinity for the members of their assigned group and then generating conflict between the groups was relatively straightforward. The conflict formed as planned at the first and third camps; at the second camp, the boys discovered the experimental set-up as the conflict was building, so Sherif cut the study short. In the end, resolving the animosity between the groups was achieved in only the last of the three camps.

Initially, the researchers arranged a series of scenarios in which the rival groups were increasingly in contact—sharing the mess hall during meal time, attending a movie together. Not only did mere exposure to one another fail to relieve the tension, in some circumstances it exacerbated the name calling and arguments between the groups. At the first camp, researchers also challenged the groups to band together to compete against an external softball team, but even this "common enemy" was only temporarily successful in creating peace between the two groups, and created new conflict aimed at a third group.

It wasn't until the researchers introduced at the 1954 camp a series of tasks with superordinate goals—problems that cannot be ignored but can only be resolved if the groups work together—that harmony rose. At that final camp, researchers arranged for the drinking water to fail, requiring the groups to team up to locate the problem with the water system. The boys shared tools and worked together across group lines, but the animosity returned when they later sat for a meal together. Researchers continued to introduce similar superordinate goals. For example, the two groups had to band together to pull-start a stalled truck that contained their meals. They were also challenged to come up with a solution that would allow them to see a movie after it was announced the camp did not have enough funds to cover the movie fee. After coming together to bring water, food, and even a movie to the camp, the lines that had been drawn between groups began to fade.

With the final of the three camps concluded and most of the boys making friends within the opposing group, Sherif and his colleagues believed they had achieved success. But would figuring out how to reduce conflict at a summer camp have an impact in the wider world?

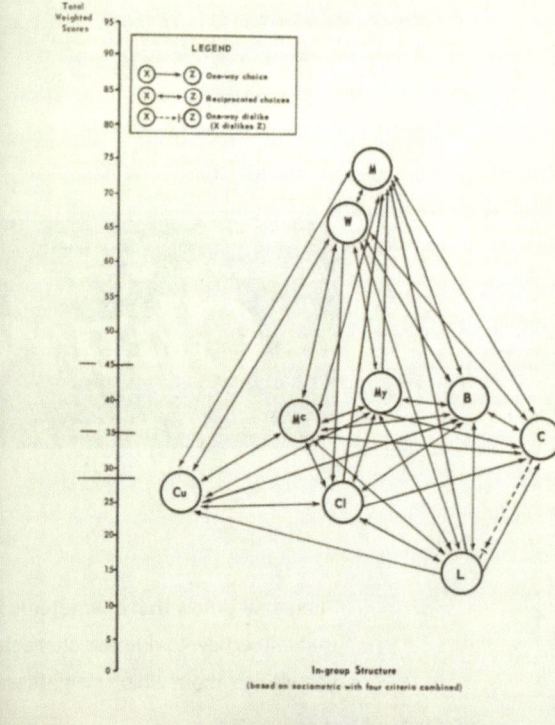

A sociogram (a diagram used to chart the relationships within a group) mapping the boys' choice of friendships at the end of the second stage of the final camp in 1954. The chart highlights an emphasis on friendships within their own group.

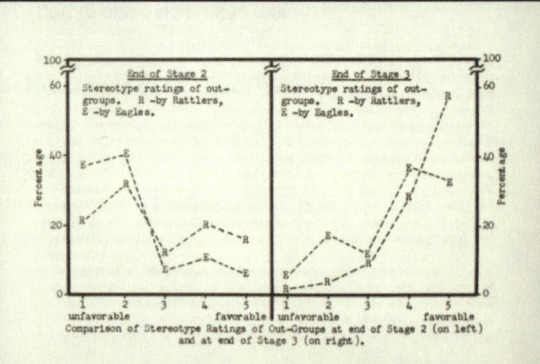

Graph of the boys' ratings of the other group divided by favorable (brave, tough, friendly) and unfavorable (sneaky, smart alecks, stinkers) terms.

Poster from the 1954 camp at Tom Hale Boy Scout Camp (Robbers Cave State Park) made by the boys following their tournament win.

The boys pull-starting a supposedly stalled food truck as part of a contrived scenario to force the two groups to work together.

One of the core tasks that brought the groups together in 1954 was an investigation into the blocked water supply, a problem staged by the research team.

At Irrational Labs, we help organizations design and grow innovative solutions that make people healthier, wealthier, and happier.

Based in San Francisco, we've worked with big names in tech (Intuit, Microsoft, LinkedIn), finance (Fidelity, Paypal, SoFi), and health (Aetna, Anthem, One Medical), as well as smaller startups to bring behavioral science into the core of product and marketing development.

We've run over 50 real-world experiments that have driven real change, and trained thousands of people in the process. Through understanding human motivations, we help build programs and solutions that influence decision-making for the better, and validate impact through rigorous testing.

Website: **irrationallabs.com**
Twitter: **@irrationallabs**

Finding Lucy in the Mind of Lennon

By Tim Kasser

When the Beatles released their album *Sgt. Pepper's Lonely Hearts Club Band* in the late spring of 1967, fans and critics alike were quick to find references to drugs throughout the LP. The album's deliriously decorated jacket featured marijuana plants in the garden behind which the Beatles stood. The lyrics of "With a Little Help from My Friends," "Lovely Rita," and "A Day in the Life" all referred to marijuana, mentioning getting "high" and taking "some tea," as well a desire to "turn you on." And tuned-in listeners easily connected the feelings, sensations, and visions people typically experience while on hallucinogenic drugs to the dreamlike imagery of "Lucy in the Sky with Diamonds." Some clever listeners even pointed out that the song's title shares the initials of the hallucinogen LSD (lysergic acid diethylamide).

The Beatles had no doubt contributed to the perception that *Sgt. Pepper* was indeed a piece of hippie propaganda for hallucinogenic partying. Around the time the album was released, Paul McCartney revealed in a *Life* magazine interview that he had been using marijuana and LSD. McCartney even went on to extol the virtues of LSD, claiming that it had brought him closer to God and would yield world peace if only politicians would try it. Soon after, John Lennon, George Harrison, and the Beatles' manager Brian Epstein also admitted that they had used LSD. Later that summer, the Beatles endorsed the legalization of marijuana by signing their names to a full-page advertisement in the *London Times*.

Despite these public proclamations about his drug use, John Lennon steadfastly denied that "Lucy in the Sky with Diamonds" was about drugs. Lennon instead consistently claimed that the song was a response to a picture painted by his almost four-year-old son Julian. The oft-repeated story goes that Julian had brought the picture home from school and told his father that it was of his friend, Lucy, who was up in the sky with diamonds. Lennon's mind had then wandered toward the Lewis Carroll books *Alice in Wonderland* and *Through the Looking-Glass* that he had long admired and recently been re-reading. "Lucy in the Sky with Diamonds" was born when Lennon took images from Julian's picture and combined them with elements of Carroll's stories and poems.

A third explanation for the song's meaning and origin was provided by Lennon many years after it was written, just a few weeks before he was killed. While reflecting on each of the songs in his discography, Lennon said this about "Lucy in the Sky with Diamonds":

> There was also the image of the female who would someday come save me—a 'girl with kaleidoscope eyes' who would come out of the sky. It turned out to be Yoko, though I hadn't met Yoko yet.... The imagery was Alice in the boat. And also the image of this female who would come and save me—this secret love that was going to come one day. So it turned out to be Yoko, though, and I hadn't met Yoko then. But she was my imaginary girl that we all have.

Lennon's 1980 explanation provided the springboard for yet another interpretation of the song. In a footnote to his 1994 book, *Revolution in the Head: The Beatles' Records and the Sixties*, music critic Ian MacDonald suggested the following:

> The "girl with kaleidoscope eyes" ... was, for Lennon, the lover/mother of his most helpless fantasies: "the image of the female who would someday come save me." This mysterious, oracular woman—mourned for in "Yes It Is" [Lennon's 1965 recording], bewildered by in "She

Said, She Said" [Lennon's 1966 song]—was originally his mother, Julia, a role subsequently assumed by Yoko Ono [in the song "Julia," Lennon's 1968 recording].

So here we have four explanations for the origin and meaning of "Lucy in the Sky with Diamonds": (1) It is about the drug LSD; (2) it is a lyrical response to Julian's drawing, colored by the writings of Lewis Carroll; (3) it is about a female savior who turned out to be Yoko Ono; and (4) it is about Lennon's mother, Julia. Is only one of these explanations true? Are none of them true? Are they all true?

My sense is that while all of these explanations have some appeal, each one by itself is incomplete and only partially satisfying.

Given the array of potential explanations that have been provided for the meaning of "Lucy in the Sky with Diamonds," and the limitations of each explanation, perhaps it is not surprising that Stephen Spignesi and Michael Lewis offered a fifth approach to the song in their book *Here, There, and Everywhere*: "Is there an ultimate meaning to the song? Not empirically: The observation of the song's 'reality' does not provide answers."

The problem with this statement is that, to my knowledge, an empirical observation of the song's reality has not yet been fully attempted. Previous explanations have provided rather superficial descriptions of the event that inspired the song's creation, unsubstantiated speculations about the role of drugs and women in its composition, and an introspective explanation by the song's author, who perhaps should not be fully trusted. Empirical data might shed light on the song's meaning, as well as on its place in Lennon's psyche.

Linguistic Analysis of "Lucy in the Sky with Diamonds"

The idea that linguistic style reflects both people's personalities and their current psychological states has been written about at great length by many psychologists over the decades. More contemporary psychological research on the topic has benefited from a computer program developed by Dr. James Pennebaker at the University of Texas at Austin.

This program, Linguistic Inquiry and Word Count (LIWC), quickly scans through a text of any length and searches out words that have been shown to be reliable indicators of around 70 preset categories. These categories include pronouns, verb tense, cognitive activity, and emotional words, but also prepositions (e.g., "over" and "under") and articles (e.g., "a" and "the"), words that concern space (e.g., "down") and time (e.g., "hour"), words that refer to discrepancies (e.g., "would" or "should"), and many others. Some words are classified by the LIWC computer program as simultaneously belonging to multiple categories. For example, words such as "laughed" would be classified as an "emotion," a "positive emotion," and a "past tense verb." After scanning through and categorizing a text, the LIWC program presents the user with information about the percentage of words that fall into each category.

This research literature shows that that the linguistic style used in a particular piece of writing or speech is influenced by features of the author's personality (e.g., whether one is depressed and suicidal), by the author's current situation (e.g., whether one is lying, whether one is addressing an authority figure), and even by current societal events (e.g., whether one's country has just suffered a terrorist attack). For this reason, merely running the LIWC program on "Lucy in the Sky with Diamonds" is unlikely to reveal anything very useful, as there would be no way to sort out how much the song's linguistic style was influenced by Lennon's personality, by his psychological situation at the time he was writing the song, or by the general era in which the song was recorded.

What is needed, therefore, is a group of songs whose linguistic styles can be compared to that of "Lucy in the Sky with Diamonds." I collected two such groups of comparison songs: the lyrics to other songs that Lennon had recorded in the previous year or so, and the lyrics to the no. 1 hit songs in the United States and the United Kingdom between January of 1966 and February of 1967.

I then compared the LIWC scores for "Lucy in the Sky with Diamonds" to these two samples of songs. If the linguistic style of "Lucy in the Sky with Diamonds" is basically similar to the linguistic styles of the songs in these two com-

Rather than expressing the bevy of emotions that typically occur while one is tripping ... "Lucy in the Sky with Diamonds" is almost barren of feeling.

parison groups, it would suggest that "Lucy in the Sky with Diamonds" was little different than other songs of the era and reflected nothing particularly special about Lennon's personality or about his psychological state at the time he was writing this particular song. If the linguistic style of "Lucy in the Sky with Diamonds" is different from the no. 1 hit songs but similar to other songs Lennon had recently been writing, it would suggest that the song's linguistic style mostly reflects Lennon's personality. Finally, if the linguistic style of "Lucy in the Sky with Diamonds" differs from the songs in both of these comparison groups, it would suggest that something about Lennon's psychological state at the time he was writing this particular song was primarily responsible for its linguistic style.

The results of the LIWC analysis show many ways in which the linguistic style of "Lucy in the Sky with Diamonds" is not especially different from the styles of the songs in the comparison groups. For example, the song is fairly typical in terms of its use of second and third person pronouns, and in its use of words concerning family, friends, achievement, money, religion, and the like. In these ways, the song appears to be typical of the songs Lennon and other musicians were writing during that era.

At the same time, there are numerous LIWC indicators on which "Lucy in the Sky with Diamonds" consistently differs both from songs Lennon had recently written and from other popular songs of the time. My understanding of the findings led me to classify these differences into three groups of indicators, as shown in Table 1.

The first group of indicators includes linguistic features that parallel what many people report experiencing when they take the drug LSD. For example, the cardinal feature of the drug experience is the presence of vivid visual hallucinations, in which colors and patterns seem to move through space and stable objects change their form unexpectedly. These types of experiences seem to be well-represented in "Lucy in the Sky with Diamonds," as it scores consistently higher than many other popular songs of the era and songs Lennon had recently written in the percentage of words that concern *seeing* (e.g., "picture" and "eyes"), *motion* (e.g., "follow" and "drift"), and *space* ("in" and "down"). The song is also rather lower than these other songs in words that convey *certainty* (e.g., "always" and "never"). Certainty is often in doubt while people are under the influence of LSD, given how the drug changes their perceptual experiences.

Users of LSD also often report what is known as an "oceanic feeling," a blissful experience in which the boundaries between themselves and others become less distinct, resulting in a feeling of connectedness with everyone and everything in the universe. These feelings of connection and the dissolution of boundaries are perhaps expressed in the song's lyrics through the high use of *inclusive* words (like "and" and "with") and the relative lack of *exclusive* words (like "but" and "without"). It is also tantalizing to note that, just as people typically take LSD by swallowing a small piece of paper infused with the chemical, words concerning *ingestion* (e.g., "eat" and "pies") occur more frequently in "Lucy in the Sky with Diamonds" than in the comparison songs.

While these findings are no doubt excellent fodder for those who claim that "Lucy in the Sky with Diamonds" is primarily about the experience of taking LSD, the song's linguistic style has other interesting linguistic features that suggest the song is not just "an acid song." In fact, five of the linguistic indicators on which "Lucy in the Sky with Diamonds" stands out map almost exactly onto one of the fundamental dimensions of linguistic style, called *immediacy vs. distancing*. This dimension indexes the extent to which a person's language reflects being present in the here and now vs. separating oneself from what is happening at a particular moment.

Research using the LIWC program has identified five specific linguistic features that cluster together to represent how immediate vs. distant a particular verbal expression is. More immediate language uses *first person singular words* (like "I" and "me") and *present tense* words (like "am" and "run"), whereas distanced language avoids such words, presumably in an attempt to direct one's awareness away from the experience of the moment. The third linguistic indicator includes words that imply a *discrepancy* (like "would" or "should"). Immediate language uses such words, as they often relate some other state to the present (e.g., "I should have bought an apple instead of this candy bar"), whereas distanced language tends to avoid discrepancies. Immediate language also uses few *articles* (e.g., "a" and "the"), whereas distanced language uses many. This is probably because articles occur alongside concrete nouns (like "a river" or "the shore") that usually make reference to something outside of oneself. Finally, immediate language uses *shorter, simpler* words whereas distanced language uses longer, more complicated words (like "plasticine" and "tangerine"); this tendency likely reflects the fact that people often use abstractions and intellectualized language to avoid awareness of what they are actually experiencing in the moment.

What is remarkable about the LIWC results for "Lucy in the Sky with Diamonds" is that for each of these five indicators, the song consistently scores in the direction of being distanced rather than immediate. That is, compared both to other recent Lennon songs and to other recent popular songs, the lyrics of "Lucy in the Sky with Diamonds" have a relatively low percentage of first-person singular pronouns, present tense verbs, and discrepant words, and a relatively high percentage of long words and of articles. Indeed, when I computed a summary score following the standard LIWC formula for combining these five indicators, the results showed that "Lucy in the Sky with Diamonds" is more distanced and less immediate than any of the songs Lennon had written in the previous year and than any of the no. 1 hits of the era.

The finding that "Lucy in the Sky with Diamonds" is a very distanced and nonimmediate song is also consistent with the last set of indicators I will mention here: words expressing emotion and feeling. "Lucy in the Sky with Diamonds" is almost stripped of emotion according to the LIWC results. Only 0.44 percent of the words in

the lyrics convey positive emotion, and there are no words that the LIWC program recognizes as conveying negative emotion. The song also has no *feeling* words, i.e., words that reflect a bodily sense of connection to one's inner world (e.g., a gut feeling) or to the outer world (e.g., a caress or a punch). Both of these findings stand in contrast to the fact that while people are under the influence of LSD, they often report relatively strong emotions, both of the pleasant and not-so-pleasant varieties.

In some ways, the results of the LIWC analysis can be seen as consistent with the common claim that "Lucy in the Sky with Diamonds" is about the drug LSD. But instead of reflecting the deep involvement in one's subjective experience and feelings that are typical of taking LSD, the lyrics of "Lucy in the Sky with Diamonds" are actually more similar to how people write and speak when they are lying and when they are attempting to psychologically distance themselves from painful psychological material. Rather than focusing on the experience of the here and now, the lyrics of the song avoid the self and the present, and instead focus on the abstract, the intellectual, and that which is outside of one's self. Moreover, rather than expressing the bevy of emotions that typically occur while one is tripping, and that Lennon often expressed in his other songs, "Lucy in the Sky with Diamonds" is almost barren of feeling. Emotions, of course, are notoriously "here and now," and rarely abstract. These analyses suggest that while Lennon was writing these lyrics, he may have been rather wary of engaging the present moment, his own inner experience, and his emotions. ∎

Excerpted from Lucy in the Mind of Lennon. *Copyright © 2013 Oxford University Press. Reprinted by permission of Oxford University Press through PLSclear. All rights reserved.*

Tim Kasser is emeritus professor of psychology at Knox College, where he taught for 24 years. His work focuses on materialism, values, ecological sustainability, and quality of life, among other topics. He is the author of *The High Price of Materialism* and *Lucy in the Mind of Lennon.*

TABLE 1

LIWC Indicator	Compared to Contemporary Lennon Songs	Compared to Contemporary No. 1 Songs in the UK and US
Typical of LSD Trip		
Seeing	Somewhat High	Somewhat High
Motion	Somewhat High	Somewhat High
Space	Extremely High	Extremely High
Certainty	Somewhat Low	Low
Inclusive	Extremely High	Extremely High
Exclusive	Somewhat Low	Low
Ingestion	Somewhat High	High
Immediacy vs. Distancing		
> 6 Letters	High	Extremely High
First person singular pronouns	Somewhat Low	Very Low
Articles	High	Extremely High
Present tense verbs	Low	Very Low
Discrepancy	Somewhat Low	Somewhat Low
Emotions		
Total Affect (Emotion)	Somewhat Low	Somewhat Low
Feeling	Somewhat Low	Somewhat Low

Sound Becomes Immortal

By Ainissa Ramirez

In 1977, as Steven Spielberg was putting the finishing touches on *Close Encounters of the Third Kind*, a movie in which humans use musical notes to communicate with aliens, NASA was preparing its own message to share with extraterrestrials, too. That year, the space agency had a once-in-a-lifetime opportunity with the launching of its two Voyager spacecrafts, for they would be able to travel faster and farther than originally conceived. The planets were lining up in a unique geometry that happened only every 176 years, and in this formation, one planet could toss a spacecraft to the next planet and then the next, like a hot potato. By using the gravity of the planets, these space vehicles could be slingshot across the solar system, using less fuel but acquiring great speeds, reaching the farthest of distances and possibly alien worlds.

Accompanying these Voyager spacecrafts would be a message, but not just an ordinary one. The contents would be historic, representing a culture like an early map or a carving on a cave wall. The magnitude of the message was great because calculations showed that the Voyager crafts would be able to travel unimpeded for billions of years, outliving Earth itself. With that, these twin Voyager spaceships were promoted from being just space probes to being the last artifacts of human life, carrying a parcel of Earth's last data.

The idea for the space message culminated a year earlier, in 1976, when John Casani, the project manager of the Voyager mission, contacted Cornell astronomy professor Carl Sagan and asked him to come up with some kind of message to attach to the spacecrafts. Sagan said, "Absolutely."

Sagan decided on sending a record. Unlike a vinyl disc, a recording medium that was popular on Earth in the 1970s, this record was going to be a 12-inch gold-coated copper disc. The Golden Record, as it was called, for each of the twin voyager rocket launches would contain greetings from Earth, images, sounds, and music. Sagan pulled together friends to form an ad hoc Voyager Record Committee, which included his wife, Linda Salzman Sagan; Jon Lomberg, the illustrator for Sagan's books; Timothy Ferris, a writer at Rolling Stone magazine; and, Ann Druyan, a novelist and Ferris's fiancé. Each member handled different parts of the record's contents, but all of them contributed to the music.

Selecting the music for the 90 minutes of playing time designated to represent the entire Earth had technical challenges as well as human ones. Before the age of digital files, music resided on physical discs and cassettes, which had to be located in the bins at Tower Records and other music stores and then manually carried to the studio to be played. In addition to these technical difficulties, there was the challenge of selecting what to send into space. Music selections touched the personal, such that individual taste became a guiding force, unlike the impersonal math that made the space trajectories possible. For members of the Voyager Record Committee, being Noah for a space ark strummed a human chord. Unknowingly, their judgment for musical selections was being clouded by bias, too.

Most of the songs originally selected for the Golden Record were classical music, a genre of which Sagan was a fan, originating from a small region of Europe, and not the whole blue pale dot, as Sagan loved to call Earth. Slowly, however, the selections began to include music from other cultures. With the urging of the younger members of the team, the suggestions from an anthropologist, and the chiding and prodding by legendary song hunter Alan Lomax, minds were swayed and the playlist began to reflect the entire planet. Soon, the Golden Record was a true sampling of the place from where it came. Beethoven's Fifth Symphony, with its iconic first notes that rip open the silence of space, was also accompanied by Senegalese percussion, Azerbaijani flutes, Navajo chants, Melanesian panpipes, and African-American jazz.

With one Golden Record blasting from Earth on August 20 and the other on September 5, 1977, their long journeys as Earth's mixtapes began. NASA's mission had the initial intention of collecting data about space, but it also dispatched data—the world's music. This event in 1977 was made possible by an invention created exactly 100 years earlier—the phonograph.

In 1877, Thomas Edison, on a fluke, created a contraption that would be important to society, for it made possible not only the storing of music but also the ability to share it. Today, our modern sensibilities cannot imagine a world where music is not available on the ready, but it once wasn't. In order for music to be easily accessible, it had to go through a metamorphosis. Music had to change its shape. It had to become physical. Music had to become data.

Before 1877, no machine could record and play back a human voice. As such, the pitch and cadence of anyone who died before Edison's innovation were unknowable. Generations would never be familiar with Confucius's voice or Shakespeare's. Generations would never know the sound of Abraham

Thomas Edison with an early phonograph circa 1878.

ORIGINAL PHOTO: Levin C. Handy.

In order for music to be easily accessible, it had to go through a metamorphosis ... It had to become physical.

Lincoln's voice or Frederick Douglass's. Generations would never learn how Poe or Dickinson actually read their work. Even the pronunciation of ancient languages, like the spoken language represented by Egyptian hieroglyphics, would elude scholars forever. The capturing of sound before the nineteenth century was a formidable task, a dream parallel to lassoing light or bottling a breeze. The poet Ralph Waldo Emerson foresaw Edison's technology when he wrote, "We shall organize the echo." But in 1877, Edison did more than just organize echoes. He made them tangible and portable and able to be played back.

In the summer of 1877, 31-year-old Thomas Edison was catapulting technologies of the nineteenth century into the future and had his eyes set on two inventions. In his lab and in his musings, he wanted to make a way to automatically write telegraph messages from Samuel Morse's invention, and he wanted to fix a flaw in Alexander Graham Bell's telephone. It was while working on both the telephone and telegraph on July 17, 1877, that the idea of combining them, like peanut butter and chocolate, came to him. By merging the ability to write from the telegraph and the capacity to receive sound from the telephone, Edison devised what he later called his favorite creation, a machine with the capability to write sound. He called it the phonograph.

The summer months of 1877 were hectic as Edison tried to make a better telephone to catch up with Alexander Graham Bell's popular product invented the year before, as well as keep pace with the flood of ideas from his own head. One section of his long-roomed laboratory contained tables full of springs, levers, and sharp tips to make a machine that pricked dots and dashes into strips of paper with special coatings as a way to record messages from Morse's telegraph. In another part of the room, Edison was also experimenting with the telephone. Although Alexander Graham Bell had beaten him, Bell's design had problems. Whenever words with consonants of t, p, v, and c were spoken, they hissed; the sounds "s" "th" and "sh" were inaudible. Every day, Edison's workers found him yelling into a cone-shaped mouthpiece with his fingers on the back, feeling the vibrations in the thin material over the narrow part of the cone, called a diaphragm. Edison tested several candidates for this material to find which one faithfully trembled with a human voice. His notebooks swelled with drawings, as his entries pitched between the telephone and the telegraph. It was in the course of these hot and humid days of intense thinking, surrounded by parts that pricked paper and slices of resonating slivers, that his idea hatched.

During an ordinary midnight dinner, when the activity in the beehive of Edison's laboratory momentarily paused, the Wizard of Menlo Park, his shaggy hair pointing in all directions, was still working on his quivering materials. Thinking out loud, he stated an idea to his chief assistant, Charles Batchelor, with his legendary overconfidence. "If we put a point on the center of that diaphragm and talked to it whilst we pulled the wax paper underneath," he said, "it would give us back talking when we pulled the paper through the second time." His idea hit everyone in the laboratory like a thunderclap.

Instruments resting on the wooden tables from some of Edison's earlier projects were immediately pilfered and repurposed. One person cut off the sharp tip of a needle and soldered it to a circular diaphragm. Another person fastened the diaphragm and mouthpiece to a wooden stand. Yet another cut a strip of wax-coated paper and placed it under the diaphragm's needle. In less than an hour, an apparatus appeared before the wizard. The room quieted as Edison sat down, leaned his portly frame forward, and nested his lips onto the mouthpiece. He then yelled, "Halloo," as his assistant Batchelor pulled the strip of waxed paper underneath slowly and evenly, like fishing line in a pond. When Edison stopped shouting into the horn, he and Batchelor looked at the paper and noticed the line was wide and then narrow, like a digesting earthworm's physique. The two put the paper back where it started and pulled it under the diaphragm again. "I listened breathlessly," said Edison. "We heard a distinct sound," he said, "which a strong imagination might have translated into the original 'Halloo!'" The nearly deaf Edison heard something, but Batchelor was skeptical.

Months passed, and even though Edison could not get back to the phonograph, he kept drawing designs in his notebook. At the end of November, he found time to think about his machine, deciding on using a cylinder to store a voice after considering both a disc and a long strip of paper. The genius of his design was its simplicity: a mouthpiece collected the sound waves, which pushed the diaphragm, like a trampoline, and a sharp tip attached to the diaphragm moved up and down, pricking the tinfoil wrapped around a cylinder. After much thought and a few different iterations, the Thursday after Thanksgiving Edison sketched his design and passed it to his trusty machinist, John Kruesi, and told him of his intention to make a machine that talked. Kruesi looked at him incredulously.

Kruesi, in a machining marathon, spent the first six days of December making the phonograph. While bringing Edison's idea to life, Kruesi engraved a spiral groove around the brass cylinder, like a candy-cane stripe, to provide a track to guide the needle as it traveled, and also to make legroom for the sharp tip to push into the foil. He, along with Charles Batchelor, attached the tinfoil to the cylinder, before passing it on to their boss for testing on December 6. The wizard then hovered his lips over the mouthpiece and prepared to give his brainchild its first words. Uttering what Edison often said to his young children, nicknamed "Dot" and "Dash," he shouted, "Mary had a little lamb." When another speaker cone was attached and the crank was turned, Edison's words came out faintly, but undeniably. "I was never so taken aback in my life," he said.

Admittedly, his invention was flawed. The words "Mary had a little lamb" probably sounded like "ary ad ell am" on the first try. Additionally, the phonograph could hold less than a minute of sound, limited by the length of the helical groove on the cylinder; and, because of the softness of tin, the message could only be played two or three times before the metal deformed and eroded the sound beyond the point of being decipherable. Nevertheless, Edison's enthusiasm never waned as he and his men toiled all night in making the phonograph as articulate as possible. They wanted to show their creation to the world the next day.

On December 7, 1877, Edison and Batchelor boarded the train from the tiny wood platform in Menlo Park, New Jersey, to head to New York City and were joined by Edison's business associate Edward Johnson to visit the offices of *Scientific American*, the premier source of science news. There, they placed the phonograph on the editor's desk as a few onlookers gathered. Edison turned the crank, and the growing crowd, making the floor creak, heard "Good Morning. How are you doing? How do you like the phonograph?" and then the phonograph bid the crowd a good night. *Scientific American* did something it rarely did. It stopped the presses that day to alert all of humanity that life had changed. "Speech has become," they said, "immortal."

Edison created a new way to represent information in addition to written language. Words on a page had two lives—a spoken existence and a written one. But sound only had one life to live. Sound was confined to a short time span and a habitat confined between one person's lips and another's ears. Beyond these bounds, sound, like a snowflake, left no signature. For these reasons, when Edison spoke "Mary Had a Little Lamb" into his phonograph, his words were a milestone of human progress equivalent to Neil Armstrong's "One small step for man, one giant leap for mankind" while stepping onto the moon. With the phonograph, utterances like a baby's first words could be heard and cherished at any time. Without Edison—or humanity—realizing it, however, Edison changed the shape of data. Information had undergone a metamorphosis, from scribbles on parchment and words stamped on paper with Gutenberg's printing press to Edison's pricks in tin.

The Wizard of Menlo Park had a vision for his favorite invention, and a few months after he created it, he made a list of predictions for the uses of his brainchild. They included audiobooks, educational lessons, last testimonies, music, toys, and answering machines, many of which exist today. Edison also believed the primary use for his invention would be dictation for business. Here, he was wrong, for where the phonograph would leave its mark was in music.

Before the phonograph, the diffusion of songs was made possible by live performances of traveling singing troupes or with sheet music played by local talent. The phonograph ignited the nation's imagination and would soon be found in the furthest outskirts of civilization, from the plushest parlor of wealthy homes to the most decrepit houses of the poorest farmers, democratizing the listening of music. Edison's dream was that with his phonograph, any person from any walk of life could have a song. And, with his invention, everyone did.

The wizard brought music into people's lives, and before long, how society experienced music changed. During a live performance, music was a shared event in a concert hall or park or juke joint between performers and the audience, and between audience members with each other. With the phonograph, the collective musical experience shrank from large halls to living rooms, but the trade-off was that the music could now be played at any time. The phonograph was one of Edison's favorite inventions, but not everyone was a fan of Edison's phonograph. John Philip Sousa, the patron saint for marching bands, believed the phonograph would bring "a marked deterioration in American music and musical taste." Yet the sales of phonographs grew. By 1906, 30 years after Edison's invention, over 26 million records were sold. Fifty years later, by 1927, record sales were 100 million.

The public found music from the phonograph to be irresistible, but they might not have known that the phonograph was shaping the music they enjoyed along the way. Just as Alexander Graham Bell's early telephone could not pick up sounds like "s" and "sh," Edison's phonograph was similarly limited. Cellos, violins, and guitars produced tones too soft for the early phonograph to pick up, so louder instruments like pianos, banjos, xylophones, tubas, trumpets, and trombones became preferred for recordings of music. Additionally, phonographs helped to fashion musical styles in a nation that was highly segregated. Blacks and whites did not socialize, but phonograph records crossed these racial divides, enabling white and Black musicians to hear and borrow styles from one another. Phonographs were dispatches of culture. This sharing of music between these musicians helped fashion jazz and blues and later rock and roll, creating a cohesion of society that Edison could never have predicted. ∎

Excerpted from The Alchemy of Us, *Chapter 6, by Ainissa Ramirez. Copyright © 2020 by Ainissa Ramirez. Reprinted by permission of The MIT Press. All rights reserved.*

Ainissa Ramirez, an award-winning scientist and science communicator, is the author of *The Alchemy of Us*, which was a *Los Angeles Times* Book Prize finalist. Ramirez is a graduate of Brown University and earned her Ph.D. in materials science and engineering from Stanford. She began her career at Bell Labs and held academic positions at MIT and Yale University.

BVA Nudge Consulting is proud to be a supporting partner of *Behavioral Scientist*.

BVA Nudge Consulting is a global consultancy that combines behavioral science and sectoral expertise to help organizations drive successful behavior change, build enduring capabilities, and deliver measurable results. We've conducted hundreds of successful engagements to help clients (such as BNP Paribas, Bristol Myers Squibb, Reckitt Benckiser, the French government, and the United Nations) learn, apply, and instill behavioral science into their core operations—and to create transformative change among their customers and within their own organizations. Our recent projects have involved:

- Reducing disparities in access to medical treatment among marginalized communities
- Helping a railway reduce delays caused by passenger behavior, by nudging more efficient boarding of trains and proper use of the emergency button
- Applying behavioral science to increase diversity and inclusion at a bank, and training financial advisors to promote female financial participation
- Developing a behavioral science learning and coaching platform for global organizations

BVA Nudge Consulting is passionate in applying behavioral science for good in the private sector, in areas including sustainability, DEI, health and safety, and digital adoption. We are also committed to innovation, thought leadership, and knowledge sharing across the behavioral science community, through our books, articles, webinars, and BE Good podcast.

Learn more at **bvanudgeconsulting.com**
Download our new book, *Applying & Infusing Behavioral Science: A Guide for Behavioral Science Champions*, at **bvanudgeconsulting.com/book**

When It All Became Apparent

By Ariel Kalil, Susan E. Mayer, and Michelle Park Michelini

"**B**ecause I said so!" Ariel yelled at her youngest when he asked why he had to go to bed. In the office the next morning, Ariel mentioned to Susan that she felt bad for how she had reacted. To Ariel this was authoritarian-style parenting and anathema to how nearly every developmental scientist believes a good parent should behave.

Susan didn't see it that way. "You said it was bedtime and it was bedtime. What's so bad about that?"

For over 50 years scholars have relied on a taxonomy of parenting styles that sorts parents into buckets labeled authoritarian, authoritative, permissive, or neglectful based on how they interact with their children. If Jamie lies, does his mother punish him, put him in time out, or let it go? If Emma does a good job sharing, does her father ignore it or praise her?

The idea of parenting styles originated in 1960s discussions about child-rearing, and the taxonomy aimed to identify the basic elements of successful parenting. In the ensuing decades, the idea that one of these styles produced accomplished, socially competent kids, while the others did not, took root in the academic literature and the popular imagination. The authoritative style was the clear winner.

Whereas the authoritarian parent is akin to a dictator in the parent-child relationship, the authoritative parent is supportive and tuned in to their child, sets clear rules and expectations (and follows through on them), and applies flexible, nonpunitive consequences to rule breaking and noncompliant behavior. The idea that authoritative parenting is the best parenting continues to dominate popular advice as well as developmental psychology. But there is one key problem.

The morning Ariel complained to Susan about being too authoritarian, something crystalized for us. The idea of parenting styles has been so embedded in the thinking of scientists, parents, and educators alike that we took it for granted. Labeling parenting styles implied that researchers could forecast how kids raised with different types of parents would turn out. But the problem was that there was little compelling causal evidence that one style was better than another. In fact, we did not even have a consensus about objectively measuring different styles. And we lacked evidence about how to help parents adopt and sustain a new style of parenting. We had been lulled into a false sense of understanding of one of the fundamental pillars of society.

As social scientists, the realization that we, both as parents and as society, are drawing conclusions about something as consequential as child development with little basis in evidence is a call to action. So we set out to help find out scientifically what parent behaviors, rather than style, matter most for children's success.

Raising a child is fundamentally a series of decisions, big and small, made every day that sum to the thing we call "parenting." Whether it's getting your child to school, reading to your child, or helping them learn math, parents constantly make decisions that affect their children. We decided to focus our research on how parents make decisions about their children and what decisions matter the most.

What we've found is that in most situations, parents generally know what decisions they ought to make. In our surveys, parents tell us that they know that reading books will improve their children's reading skills and that spending time doing math activities will improve their child's math skills. Parents also say that they find joy and meaning in spending time with their children during these activities. The problem is that some parents chronically make decisions about their child that are out of step with what they know is beneficial for their child and say they want to do.

This is both good and bad news. The bad news is that parents, when making decisions about their kids, are subject to the same cognitive barriers that often prevent us from making optimal decisions in other areas of our lives, from our finances to our fitness. We can be shortsighted, influenced by present bias, and swayed by things like stress, distraction, and mood. The stakes are high when we fail to make the best decisions about our money or health, but they're even higher when we fail to do so as parents. Parents are decision makers whose choices are far-reaching both for individual human development and collective societal well-being.

The good news is that it is possible to help parents close the gap between their intended and actual decisions. For instance, we know we can help parents follow through on their intentions by first helping them recognize they are making decisions all the time that have a long-run impact on their children's future. Framing parenting as a series of important decisions shifts parents' focus from the personal dynamics or style of their interactions with their child to the decisions they make for their child.

Parents should know that perfection is not the goal, and it is not going to ruin their children if they occasionally skip dinner for dessert, go to bed without brushing their teeth, or miss out on extra math for a movie. Admittedly, our kids have eaten neon cereal straight from the box in lieu of lunch, and we've skipped the book reading for the night because we could not stand to read *Hop on Pop* one more time.

Rather, it is what we as parents do with regularity that matters the most. With that in mind, we can work to find out which behavioral tools support parents in setting and meeting goals for their decisions. When reminders are effective and when they're not. Who planning prompts help the most and why. When bedtime means "now" and when that boundary can be porous.

As our lab and others continue to research what matters for children's success, we can keep Ariel's aha moment in mind. Scientists are humans too, and when it comes to parenting, we are subject to the same cognitive barriers and biases as everyone else. We can be captivated by comfortable narratives rather than rigorous evidence, and we can fail to follow through too often on what we know is in our children's best interest. The science, like children, and like parents, is a work in progress. ■

Ariel Kalil is the Daniel Levin professor at the University of Chicago Harris School of Public Policy. At Harris, she directs the Center for Human Potential and Public Policy and co-directs the Behavioral Insights and Parenting Lab.

Susan E. Mayer is a professor and dean emeritus at the University of Chicago Harris School of Public Policy, where she co-directs the Behavioral Insights and Parenting Lab.

Michelle Park Michelini is the executive director of the Behavioral Insights and Parenting Lab at the University of Chicago Harris School of Public Policy.

CHAPTER 5

Mastering Two Worlds

"My imagination makes me human and makes me a fool; it gives me all the world and exiles me from it."

—URSULA K. LE GUIN

Behavioral Science in the Backcountry

The Decades-Long Quest to Overcome "The Human Factor" in Avalanche Deaths

By Greg Rosalsky

On a stormy Sunday in February 1995, 37-year-old Steve Carruthers strapped on his skis and headed into the Wasatch Mountains near Salt Lake City, Utah. It had dumped almost two feet of snow that weekend, and Carruthers and two friends wanted to ski powder in the untamed wilderness of the backcountry. The Utah Avalanche Center's advisory warned there was a serious danger of avalanches that day. The new snow, it cautioned, had fallen on a slippery crust of ice, and steeper slopes could slide. But these skiers were seasoned veterans, and they believed they could avoid trouble.

The three skiers cut through a thick morning fog, gliding past the evergreen conifers and leafless aspens of Big Cottonwood Canyon and began climbing the southeast face of a 10,246-foot peak called Gobblers Knob. They all had skied the area countless times. They all had beacons, shovels, and probes, the standard safety equipment for finding and extricating victims buried by avalanches. And they all knew to avoid slopes steeper than 30 degrees, the crucial threshold when slopes start becoming steep enough to slide.

Despite their experience, equipment, and training, however, the trio failed to recognize an obvious hazard. While the shallow, tree-covered slope they were ascending was not steep enough to avalanche, their route crossed under steeper terrain that could. And at about noon, the party seems to have remotely triggered an avalanche on an overhead slope. The face of the upper mountain shattered like a giant pane of glass. Within seconds, a broken slab that had been about 150 feet wide and two feet deep came rumbling towards them at around 50 miles per hour. All three were swept down the mountain by its mighty force.

The skiers' screams echoed through the canyon, and another party of skiers in the distance came rushing to help. When they arrived a half hour later, they discovered two dazed and injured men. One had only minor injuries. The other was in shock from a broken femur and risked dying of hypothermia. But they were both lucky because they had only been partially buried. They had been able to free their heads and breathe. This bought them enough time to be rescued.

Carruthers wasn't so lucky. The avalanche had rammed him into an aspen tree and buried him under two feet of snow. When the rescue party finally dug Carruthers out, they found him lifeless, with his jacket pushed over his head. He had broken ribs, a broken pelvis, and had likely asphyxiated under the frozen debris. The rescuers tried but couldn't resuscitate him. Carruthers would not be coming home that night to his wife and four-year-old daughter.

As tragic as this story is, it's made even more tragic by the fact that the story repeats itself again and again—not just in mountains all over the world but on the very same mountain where Carruthers met his fate.

In 2003, veteran backcountry skier Alan Davis died on Gobblers Knob in an avalanche that buried him under four feet of snow.

In 2007, Norwegian skier Vegard Lund, who had come to Salt Lake City to study at the University of Utah, died after an avalanche on Gobblers Knob swept him into a grove of trees.

In 2016, 49-year-old skier Douglas Green triggered an avalanche that buried him deep in a gully, killing him.

And just last year, on a peak right next to Gobblers Knob, four skiers in their twenties—Sarah Moughamian, Louis Holian, Thomas Louis Steinbrecher, and Stephanie Hopkins—all died after getting caught in a monstrous slide that was 1,000 feet wide.

In most of these cases, the skiers had significant experience, formal avalanche training, and died on days when the Utah Avalanche Center had warned of considerable avalanche danger.

As is common in the aftermath of avalanche fatalities, when Steve Carruthers died, some in his community wrote his death off, concluding he was just another careless adrenaline junkie who failed to heed warnings. But Ian McCammon knew Carruthers. They had climbed and skied together over the years. Just a couple weeks before Carruthers lost his life, McCammon bumped into him at the Utah ski resort Alta. It had been a few years since they'd spent time together, and while riding the ski lift, they reminisced and caught up.

McCammon had moved to Salt Lake City to get his Ph.D. in mechanical engineering at the University of Utah, and he met Carruthers shortly after when he got involved in the local backcountry scene. When McCammon first started skiing and climbing with Carruthers, he came to see his friend as a bit of a daredevil. But, as a lift whisked them up the mountain, Carruthers reflected on his life and told McCammon something he'd never forget.

"He told me how he had a daughter now, and how he wasn't the risk taker he used to be," McCammon says. Carruthers said that his days of heading into the mountains and making sketchy choices were over. He was a family man now, and while he still loved exploring the backcountry, his paternal instinct to always come home to his wife and daughter had greatly diminished his tolerance for risk. "And that really sat with me, and it echoed weeks later when I heard Steve died."

When McCammon got news of Carruthers's death, it really unsettled him. He was, of course, devastated to lose a friend, and he was devastated for Carruthers's family. But he was also flabbergasted by how the accident could have happened. Carruthers was an experienced backcountry skier. He had a deep knowledge of the Wasatch Mountains and the dangers of avalanches. And he had so much to live for. McCammon really believed him when he said that he was not willing to take stupid risks.

Agonizing over the tragedy, McCammon pored over the Utah Avalanche Center's accident report. He knew hindsight is twenty-twenty, but he could also see all kinds of obvious warning signs that the trio had ventured into treacherous terrain that day. The avalanche warning. The fresh snow on the ground. The topography of the area they were climbing. People had died on that same mountain before. What was going on in his friend's head as he ascended Gobblers Knob?

An avalanche may seem like an earthquake or a lightning strike or a shark attack, a random act of nature that is almost impossible to predict. But avalanche scientists have made incredible progress forecasting when and where they are most likely to occur. In most instances, the avalanches that kill people don't just happen. They are triggered. And in about 90 percent of accidents, they are triggered by the victim themself or someone in the victim's party. Most of the time, there are obvious clues that danger lurks in the snowpack.

McCammon ruminated on whether he could make similar mistakes, and he began reevaluating his whole perspective on avalanche accidents. "Up until that point, I really believed that having a good education on avalanche safety and lots of experience would be sufficient to avoid most dangers, especially when it comes to someone like Steve who had so much to live for," McCammon says. In other words, he had believed people were rational and all backcountry goers needed to stay safe was the right information. Now he wasn't so sure. "Steve's death had a profound effect on me."

Having just begun teaching avalanche safety classes at the National Outdoor Leadership School in his spare time, McCammon began to question whether he and the broader outdoor community were preparing people well enough to stay safe. Not just when it comes to teaching people about the signs of avalanche danger—but preparing them to recognize how flaws in their decision-making can lead them to ignore those signs of danger.

Although he had focused his undergraduate education on physical sciences, McCammon had encountered ideas from psychology while getting his Ph.D. in mechanical engineering. His focus was robotics and developing machines capable of making decisions, which piqued his interest in the basic psychology of decision-making. During his reading, he stumbled upon the idea that humans often rely on "heuristics," or simple rules of thumb, to quickly navigate the complexities of the world when they don't take the time to sit and think.

The concept of heuristics was developed by psychologists Daniel Kahneman and Amos Tversky back in the 1970s. It's had a huge influence on all sorts of fields. One example of a heuristic they identified is known as availability, which is when our judgments are influenced by "the ease with which instances or occurrences can be brought to mind." For instance, if you read news reports that say there haven't been any avalanche fatalities this season, that may stick in your head and influence you to underestimate the probability of snow slides, whether or not conditions change.

The snow-covered backcountry is a difficult place for human psychology.

Heuristics create a sort of autopilot for our brains, and, most of the time, they work remarkably well. But this autopilot system can steer us in directions that, in a rational state of mind, we would never want to go.

In the aftermath of Carruthers's death, McCammon dove into the psychology literature and began exploring theories and evidence for how heuristics affect human decisions. He was particularly interested in research by the psychologist Robert Cialdini on how advertising firms, cult leaders, and other antagonists exploit our heuristics and steer us where they want us to go. But the antagonist McCammon now set his sights on wasn't a person or a business. It was something lurking under the snowy face of a mountain, an invisible layer within the snowpack—"a weak layer"—which is the most common contributor to avalanche deaths.

"The mountain may not be deliberately trying to fool you," McCammon says. But lurking beneath its beautiful and tantalizing slopes is something that can. McCammon began to use the term "heuristic traps" for the faulty processes of the mind that can blind backcountry travelers to obvious dangers and lure them into peril in the mountains. While there were avalanche experts before McCammon who had recognized that human error could play a role in backcountry accidents, the avalanche community lacked rigorous research showing the severity of the problem and effective methods to try and combat it.

And so, inspired by his friend's death, McCammon began leading a double professional life. By day, he continued his career as a mechanical engineer, developing robots and aerospace systems for organizations like NASA and the Department of Defense. But at night and on weekends and days off, he began the mostly unpaid work of doing research, publishing papers, and developing tools that would revolutionize the avalanche world.

Bruce Tremper's path to becoming one of the world's foremost experts on avalanches began with an avalanche. Raised in western Montana, Tremper moved to Bozeman after undergrad and began working at Bridger Bowl Ski Area. His first job was building ski lifts. On a blustery day in November 1978, he was out alone tightening bolts on lift towers. It had snowed a foot the day before, and wind gusts were loading leeward slopes with extra snow.

After Tremper finished tightening bolts on one lift tower, he needed to reach the next one. The most direct route between the two towers crossed a 30-foot-wide couloir, a steep gully in the mountainside. He knew the couloir was avalanche terrain, so he planned to avoid it. Instead, he would climb a short distance up the mountain and make it to a ridge, circumnavigating the couloir with a safer path to the tower. But that morning, Tremper had forgotten sticky climbing skins for his skis, which backcountry skiers use to ascend in the snow, so he had to make the climb on foot. The chest-deep snow battled him every step of the way, and it quickly became clear that climbing would take too much time and effort.

Tremper, however, was an experienced ski racer. He was young. He was cocky. And he decided he could instead "ski cut" the couloir, zipping across the slope at a 45-degree angle, fast enough to outrun an avalanche if the slope did end up sliding. But as he tried to cut across the slope, he realized he had made a horrible miscalculation. He heard a muffled *thunk*, and, he says, it was like someone yanked a rug from underneath him.

The avalanche took him on a ride down the couloir before slamming him into a tiny tree. He quickly grasped the tree and held on for dear life, as a mighty river of snow moving at highway speeds flowed around him. The tree broke and he continued down the slope, gasping for air as he fought to swim above the surface. He began to brace for the worst as he submerged into the snowy torrent. But then, all of a sudden, the ferocious river stopped. Tremper's lower body was stuck in avalanche debris, but his head and arms were free. He was able to slowly chip himself out with the shovel he had in his backpack. The resort ended up naming the couloir "Tremper's," in honor of the lucky survivor.

"I wanted to learn everything I could about avalanches after that," Tremper says. "That avalanche changed my life."

Tremper went on to study avalanches at Montana State University, earning a master's degree in geology in the process. Meanwhile, he continued working at Bridger Bowl, becoming a ski patroller tasked with avalanche control. On mornings before the ski resort opened, he would strap on a pack filled with explosives and head to the resort's black diamond and double-black diamond runs, chucking bombs at the avalanche-prone slopes to clear them of deadly threats to resort guests. "I got to do all these trial-and-error experiments—and I learned so much about avalanches," he says.

After grad school and a stint as the avalanche director for Big Sky Resort, Tremper got a dream job as a backcountry avalanche forecaster at the Alaska Avalanche Forecast Center. There he got to learn from the center's head honchos, Jill Fredston and Doug Fesler, a married couple who were on their way to becoming world-renowned avalanche experts. Together they pioneered methods to teach people about avalanches that are still used today.

Before his time in Alaska, Tremper hadn't done much thinking about how humans think—and whether problems with our thinking could kill people in the backcountry. But Fredston and Fesler had spent a long time witnessing carnage in the mountains of Alaska. They saw incident after incident of skiers and snowboarders making the same stupid decisions in the face of overwhelming signs of danger. To explain why so many backcountry goers behaved like lemmings jumping into a dark abyss, Fredston and Fesler began incubating ideas that have come to be known in the avalanche community as "the human factor."

"Jill and Doug weren't social scientists, and research on the human factor was still in its infancy at the time," Tremper says. But Fredston and Fesler came to believe that there were unconscious errors in judgment that routinely led people to their death in mountainous hinterlands. They even started giving their own folksy names to the mistakes they observed, some of which behavioral scientists would call heuristics and biases. Fredston and Fesler called the tendency to blindly follow others "the sheep's syndrome." They called the rush to get the first powder tracks on a slope "the lion's syndrome."

But, Tremper says, at first he didn't buy the idea that flaws in human cognition systematically led adventurers to their peril. "I was trained in the physical sciences," he says. He saw the problem of avalanches through the lens of physics and topography and snow science. He had assumed that most deaths could be prevented by simply educating recreationists about snow dynamics. "When I was younger and coming out of graduate school, I thought people were rational."

It's hard to blame him. Tremper was like a lot of people back then, even those trained in social science. At that point, in the 1980s, most economists and many other social scientists had fallen head over heels for rational choice theory, which embraced mathematical models of human behavior in which people were perfectly rational. The implication of these models was that all people needed was information and resources, and they would always make the best choices for themselves.

But Tremper's new job as a backcountry avalanche forecaster entailed investigating avalanche accidents. And data point after data point slowly brought a startling reality of the backcountry into light. It was a reality in which skiers and snowboarders with ample avalanche training routinely died in circumstances that could have been easily predicted and avoided. Tremper, like Fredston and Fesler before him, began to have nagging doubts about the rationality of humankind. However, it wasn't until the death of his friend Mark Yates that he became fully converted.

By then, Tremper had become the director of the Utah Avalanche Center, which is based in Salt Lake City. He had hired Yates as the avalanche forecaster for the Moab area, which is on the eastern side of the state. Yates had been pretty inexperienced in avalanche forecasting at the time, but he was a Moab local and expert skier with tons of backcountry experience in the La Sal Mountains, a majestic range of snow-capped peaks that towers high above the red rocks of the Moab desert. Tremper believed Yates could grow into becoming an effective avalanche forecaster for the region.

In the winter of 1992, the Moab area spent weeks in a snow drought. In early-to-mid February, it finally began snowing again. And on February 12, the skies cleared and a couple feet of fresh snow beckoned Yates and five other skiers into the La Sal Mountains. "They were thirsty for powder," Tremper says.

The group began the day climbing a low-angle, avalanche-safe ridge up to a subsummit known as Pre-Laurel Peak. Standing at about 11,000 feet, they gazed upon an expansive winterscape glimmering in the sun. Yates was in high spirits, intoxicated by the conditions. He insisted they ski down the south face of the peak and then head into Talking Mountain Cirque, a gorgeous, upper-elevation bowl that looks like a humongous white amphitheater.

At the base of Talking Mountain Cirque, the slope is gentle, well below the 30-degree threshold where terrain can avalanche. But above that are three steep faces that can—and often do—avalanche. It was absolutely dangerous to go there in the snow conditions the skiers faced that day.

"They thought they were okay with the slope angle they were on," Tremper says. "But I know that Mark knew that you can pull these things down from below—that these collapses can propagate uphill. And when that collapse reaches terrain steep enough to slide, then it'll slide down on top of you. I mean, he *knew* that."

Two members of the group had taken an avalanche class from Tremper only weeks before. The survivors recalled these two voicing concerns about heading into Talking Mountain Cirque. They said it was a dangerous and stupid destination when there seemed to be instability in the snowpack. But Yates was the Moab avalanche forecaster. He was the alpha dog. And he kept insisting they would be okay; that they would keep traveling on gentle slopes and stay safe.

The group ultimately deferred to Yates. And, as they traveled to the cirque, they ignored all kinds of obvious clues of danger on the way. They saw evidence that a slope in the distance had already experienced a natural avalanche. They saw the snow crack underneath their skis and heard *whumpf* sounds. But, somehow, they "just kept going higher and higher into the bowl," Tremper says. "And, interestingly enough, the people who had been the most vocal that it was dangerous—they were the ones out in front, breaking trail when the whole thing came down."

The survivors recounted stopping at the precipice where the bowl started getting steep enough to slide. There, several members of the group again raised concerns about what they were doing. But it was already too late. As they stopped to talk about what to do next, they felt the snow collapse under their feet. And they heard another *whumpf*. But this telltale sound of avalanche danger was louder than the ones they heard before, reverberating through the entire amphitheater. The group looked up and saw the upper slopes all sliding. They had triggered three avalanches on three separate faces of the cirque— and two of the slides formed a V shape and were heading right towards them. They began yelling.

The avalanches completely buried and killed four of the six skiers—including Yates. It was the single most fatal avalanche accident in recorded Utah history. That is, until just this past season, when Sarah Moughamian, Louis Holian, Thomas Louis Steinbrecher, and Stephanie Hopkins all died in the Wasatch Range, near Gobblers Knob.

The Talking Mountain Cirque accident was a huge deal in Utah. Not just because it's rare for that many skiers to die at once, but because Yates was the local avalanche forecaster, and he had been traveling with a group of expert skiers who had avalanche training. It was clear they should have known better.

At the time of the accident, Tremper was actually overseas, in Japan. He had been contracted by the Japanese government to help launch an avalanche center. This was before

Bruce Tremper helped lead the movement to incorporate "human factors" into avalanche safety training.

ORIGINAL PHOTO: Bruce Tremper.

In the aftermath of Carruthers's death, McCammon began a quest to understand the cognitive errors that could lead people to their death in the backcountry.

smartphones and widespread use of the internet, so Tremper didn't hear about the accident until he returned. And when he did, the news jolted him. He began poring over the details of the accident and hearing the play-by-play from survivors.

"With that Mark Yates accident—all the things happened that Jill Fredston and Doug Fesler told me about," Tremper says. "There were all these human factors going on."

Using the terminology developed by Fredston and Fesler, Tremper could see evidence of "the lion's syndrome," or the race to get fresh powder. He could see the "sheep syndrome" when the group blindly followed Yates into trouble. He could see that Yates had been crowned as the group's expert and that the group deferred to his judgment, as flawed as it was. And Tremper could see what social scientists call confirmation bias in the group's over willingness to disregard signs of danger and confirm to themselves that their chosen route was safe.

From that point on, Tremper's view of the human factor completely changed—and he got serious about warning the avalanche community about it. "I realized that we need to start talking about human factors in our avalanche classes, addressing them specifically," Tremper says.

Within two years, he joined Jill Fredston in presenting a paper about the human factor at the International Snow Science Workshop, an annual event where avalanche experts meet and discuss ideas. They urged the group, which included officials from 11 countries, to recognize that "perception traps" could cloud backcountry travelers' judgment, and they urged educators to start talking about the human factor in avalanche courses. That year, the workshop was held at Snowbird in Utah, and Tremper recalls their presentation attracting a good amount of attention.

But Tremper also recalls many avalanche educators being hesitant to change their curricula and delve into the flaws of human psychology. "It was kind of controversial in those days because a lot of people who taught avalanche classes really didn't want to talk about it," Tremper says. "They were just like I had been. They thought people made logical decisions. They thought we just have to teach students about the science of avalanches and they'll automatically figure it out."

And that's pretty much where the avalanche community stood before Ian McCammon got involved. There was a growing awareness that human factors contributed to avalanche deaths, but most authorities weren't sure how serious the problem was and what they should do about it. Within a year of that workshop, however, Ian McCammon's friend Steve Carruthers died in circumstances similar to Yates' death. And McCammon would soon join the fight, creating a bridge between the world of avalanches and the world of social science.

In the aftermath of Carruthers's death, McCammon began a quest to understand the cognitive errors that could lead people to their death in the backcountry. And to do that, he needed data.

McCammon did not have the luxury of being able to conduct randomized experiments to prove, without a shadow of a doubt, the causes of avalanche deaths. For one thing, he didn't have the resources of a well-funded academic. But, even more fundamentally, it would be unethical to test concepts by playing with people's lives in the backcountry. He could not divide backcountry travelers into treatment and control groups by, for example, withholding essential information from one group and seeing if they were more likely to die.

Instead, McCammon had to rely on imperfect observations of the past. Avalanche professionals had long documented and archived reports of accidents, but this data had to be collected and coded to do statistical analysis. McCammon was forced to begin the long and arduous process of constructing a dataset.

Over several years, McCammon made trips to the headquarters of the Colorado Avalanche Information Center in Boulder. The CAIC maintains a historical archive that has detailed accounts of most avalanche accidents in the United States going back to 1950. Back in the late nineties, these were literally just paper reports. McCammon would camp out for days, sifting through the minute and often macabre details of accidents. He would categorize and quantify everything he could, painstakingly creating a usable dataset filled with information on the characteristics of the victims, the types of warning signs they encountered, and explanations, if any, for why they seemed to ignore these warning signs. Equipped with this dataset, which he would continue to expand in the following years, McCammon was able to do statistical analyses and find evidence for factors contributing to avalanche deaths.

One of McCammon's first studies using this dataset was published in 2000, and it investigated whether avalanche training had any effect on reducing accidents. At that time, he had a sample of 546 recreational accidents in the United States. The data wasn't perfect though. He only had information on whether the victims had avalanche training in 344 of the 546 incidents. Nonetheless, the study was one of the first times the avalanche community got a quantitative analysis suggesting behavioral problems systematically caused accidents in the backcountry.

McCammon's data suggested avalanche training did get people to mitigate risks by, for exam-

ple, increasing the likelihood they went into the backcountry with beacons, probes, and shovels. But, he found, those with formal avalanche training nonetheless seemed prone to disregard all sorts of hazards. "In fact," McCammon wrote, "victims with basic formal training exposed themselves to more hazard than any other group, including those with no awareness of avalanches."

To explain why so many backcountry goers with avalanche training overlooked obvious hazards—hazards that training aims to get people to recognize and avoid—McCammon cited Kahneman and Tversky. The psychologists, he wrote, "have demonstrated that people in difficult and unfamiliar situations base their responses on simple rules, or 'heuristics.'" When people relied on this autopilot system in their brains, McCammon warned, it could lead them into trouble. While McCammon didn't identify which specific heuristics were most problematic in the backcountry just yet, he urged avalanche educators to reform how they teach students and figure out ways to improve their "decision skills."

In 2002, McCammon's dataset had grown to include 622 accidents, and he published evidence that four specific "heuristic traps" seemed to contribute to accidents again and again: "familiarity," "social proof," "commitment," and "scarcity" (each of which will be defined below). McCammon presented his findings at the International Snow Science Workshop. For many in the audience, it was likely the first time they heard the term "heuristic." But, he says, for old timers and avalanche pros, these concepts resonated with their own experience of accidents and near-misses in avalanche terrain.

"Traditional avalanche education places a heavy emphasis on terrain, snowpack and weather factors," McCammon wrote in his 2002 paper. "While there's no doubt that this knowledge can lead to better decisions, it is disturbing that the victims in this study that were most influenced by heuristic traps were those with the most avalanche training."

In 2004, McCammon published his most influential paper, "Heuristic Traps in Recreational Avalanche Accidents: Evidence and Implications." By then, his dataset had grown to 715 accidents, and he had identified two more heuristic traps in his data that were statistically significant—"acceptance" and "expert halo." He now offered the outdoor community comprehensive evidence for six heuristic traps that likely contribute to avalanche deaths. With some creativity, he rebranded some of their names and offered a handy acronym. He called it FACETS:

F stands for familiarity. It's the tendency for people to feel safe and ignore risk factors when they're in familiar terrain. An example is thinking, "I've snowboarded this slope a dozen times, so it must be okay to do it again."

A stands for acceptance. It's when people disregard rational judgment because they want to fit in and be accepted by their group. An example is skiing a slope because your two partners want to, and you don't want to make a fuss.

C stands for commitment. After people make plans, they tend to commit to them even if the facts on the ground change. It can make them blind to obvious avalanche clues that should spur them to change course.

E stands for expert halo. It's the tendency of people to defer their judgments to someone who they consider to be an expert, even if this so-called expert may actually be reckless or stupid or just flat-out wrong about avalanche risks.

T stands for tracks. It's the tendency of skiers and snowboarders to race for fresh powder tracks. It's sometimes known as "powder fever." Social scientists call this heuristic "scarcity," but McCammon changed it to create an acronym that would be more memorable for skiers and snowboarders.

S stands for social proof. An example is the tendency of skiers and snowboarders to see tracks on a slope and assume it's safe, even though the person who created the tracks may have been an idiot who just got lucky.

More than an acronym, FACETS is a clever mnemonic device because the term is familiar to those in the avalanche community. Facets are a type of weakly bonded, sugary snow, and they're one of the leading causes of the type of avalanche that most often kills people. Facets form because of thermodynamics within the snowpack, and they create what's known as a persistent weak layer. This weak layer is what causes a slab, or a well-bonded chunk of snow, to fracture and slide (when the slope is steep enough). Snow accumulating on top of a weak layer is like a house being built on a rickety foundation. Bruce Tremper calls facets "monsters in the basement."

Faceted snow is particularly dangerous because it lurks beneath the surface. It's invisible. And so, for McCammon, FACETS is not just a pun or a handy mnemonic device for backcountry goers. It's also a metaphor for the heuristic traps that can lead people into danger. "It doesn't really matter how deep a slab is," McCammon says. "If there's a weak layer underneath the slab—it's dangerous." Similarly, he says, it doesn't really matter how deep your knowledge is of skiing or snowboarding or snowmobiling. If you're making decisions based upon faulty rules of thumb—instead of a reasoned analysis or a system designed to help you rationally process information—there's a good chance your adventures in the backcountry can become treacherous.

McCammon now offered not only statistical evidence for six common heuristics that endanger backcountry travelers. He also offered a clever way to frame these heuristics to the avalanche community, and his work proved to be a clarion call that authorities could no longer ignore. His research was soon cited all around the world. His ideas gained traction in mainstream news outlets, like *NPR*, *The New York Times*, and virtually all ski publications. Avalanche educators began incorporating the FACETS framework into their classes. And McCammon was finally able to overcome the resistance that Fredston, Fesler, and Tremper had faced when broaching the human factor. Now a critical mass in the outdoor community recognized that deep-seated flaws in human psychology could routinely lead people to their peril in the mountains.

In "The Human Factor" chapter of his popular avalanche textbook, *Staying Alive In Avalanche Terrain*, Bruce Tremper credits McCammon's FACETS framework with revolutionizing the field: "It fundamentally changed the way avalanche workers thought about avalanche accidents and how they taught their students."

But, even as McCammon was developing the FACETS framework, he didn't believe it alone would make much of a difference. In the conclusion of his 2002 paper, McCammon cited psychological research that suggested simply providing people with a list of common cognitive errors "does not make people any less susceptible to them. Thus it seems likely that effective human factors education must do more than provide a laundry list of heuristic traps: It must give people simple, viable tools for recognizing and mitigating heuristic traps and other decision errors in avalanche terrain."

So after McCammon developed his FACETS framework to get educators and backcountry goers to recognize potential flaws in decision-making, he began developing a tool to help people make better decisions when heading into the mountains. Like FACETS, this tool goes by a memorable acronym that doubles as a metaphor: ALPTRUTh, which urges backcountry adventurers to perceive the truth in the mountains.

ALPTRUTh is also known as the Obvious Clues Method. It provides backcountry travelers with a handy checklist of the seven most obvious clues of avalanche danger:

A stands for avalanches. Have there been any avalanches in the general area within the last 48 hours?

L stands for loading. Has there been any new snow, wind, or rain within the last 48 hours?

P stands for path. Are you traveling to a place with obvious avalanche paths? For example, a barren slope that is more than 30 degrees.

T stands for "terrain trap." Terrain traps are anything in the terrain that can increase the likelihood of death or injury if a slope slides. They include cliffs, trees, and gullies, all of which could be deadly if you're carried into them by even a small avalanche.

R stands for rating. It reminds backcountry goers to read their local avalanche center's daily report to see if they forecast any significant danger.

U stands for unstable snow. Have you seen or heard any cracking, collapsing, whumpfing, or any other obvious signs of instability within the snowpack?

Th stands for thaw instability. Has there been any recent warming of the snow due to sun, wind, rain, or higher air temperatures? Rapid warming contributes to the likelihood of a slope avalanching.

Using his dataset on past avalanche deaths in the United States, McCammon analyzed how many of these seven obvious clues were present in accidents before the victims got in trouble. And, he says, the average accident had five of the clues present before the avalanche.

McCammon imagined an alternate universe in which the skiers killed in avalanches had paid attention to the obvious clues in front of them and avoided avalanche terrain on the days they perished. He envisioned them using ALPTRUTh to create decision-making rules in which they picked a certain number of identifiable clues as a kind line in the snow: *if we see this number of ALPTRUTh clues today, we will turn back and not ski avalanche terrain.*

In a 2004 study, he and Pascal Haegeli crunched McCammon's dataset to figure out the most effective rule. They found that if skiers had set a rule to not ski slopes when they could identify four clues, 77 percent of them would have lived. And if skiers had set a rule of avoiding slopes when they could identify three clues, 92 percent of them would have lived.

McCammon's data may have been imperfect, but it strongly suggested that a clue-based decision aid could significantly mitigate carnage in the mountains. He saw ALPTRUTh as a kind of prototype. He hoped his research would spur others to take up the mantle and conduct more empirical analysis of how to prevent avalanche accidents. Some were skeptical of McCammon's findings, but many other researchers began following in his path.

For example, in 2012, a group of Norwegian scholars analyzed all avalanche accidents in Norway between 2005 and 2012, comparing the effectiveness of different decision-making tools. They concluded that ALPTRUTh was the most effective. They found that 50 percent of all avalanche accidents in Norway would have been avoided had skiers chosen to not ski when they could identify more than four clues. Further, they found that "100% of the accidents would have been avoided if the skier had not skied with one or two clues present."

The goal of ALPTRUTh is to get backcountry travelers to stop using faulty heuristics and emotions to make decisions in the backcountry. It urges them to instead objectively process information about avalanche danger. In other words, ALPTRUTh tries to get people to turn their brains off autopilot and think rationally about the information in front of them. In the lexicon of behavioral economists Richard Thaler and Cass Sunstein, it's a nudge. "It allows you to reframe things and get the psychological baggage out of the decision," McCammon says.

McCammon cites research by psychologist Gary Klein, who pioneered thinking on what he calls a "premortem." A postmortem, of course, is something a coroner does after someone dies to determine the cause of death. A premortem is an exercise in which people imagine a hypothetical future in which things go horribly wrong. They then use critical thinking to dissect the causes that could lead to such a disaster. Using ALP-TRUTh, McCammon says, backcountry travelers can conduct a simple premortem. Before or during your trips into the mountains, he says, you should imagine a future in which you or your partners die in an avalanche. Then look at these seven obvious clues of danger. Are they present? If they are, how stupid will your decision look if there is an avalanche?

A major advantage of ALPTRUTh, McCammon says, is that it's designed to be fast and easy. Before backcountry travelers depart on an adventure, they can run through the list of factors quickly. "You can give someone a ninety-second avalanche course in the parking lot just with these seven clues," McCammon says. "Just say: 'Look for these things, and, if you see them, be very careful about your decisions.'"

Like FACETS, ALPTRUTh has been widely embraced by the avalanche community. All kinds of outdoor organizations and companies use it to promote public safety. It inspired the creation of Avalanche Canada's portable decision-aid tool, the Avalutor, which they market to backcountry travelers. Teton Gravity Research, an extreme sports media company, and Dynafit, a maker of ski boots and clothing, have sponsored online educational videos using the acronym. Jones Snowboards offers splitboard poles with graphics of obvious red flags of avalanche danger. The American Avalanche Institute declares to the public that both ALPTRUTh and FACETS are "two acronyms that can save your life."

When Ian McCammon began publishing papers in the early 2000s, the outdoor community had witnessed a decade in which avalanche fatalities rose to scary new heights. But in the 20 years that followed, the number of fatalities stayed pretty flat, with an average of about 27 per year in the United States. At the same time, backcountry winter sports have exploded in popularity; so while the absolute number of fatalities hasn't gone down, deaths have gone down significantly on a per-capita basis. This suggests that educators are doing a better job of training adventurers how to recreate safely.

That said, the 2020/2021 winter season saw a record-breaking 37 avalanche fatalities in the United States. With the COVID-19 pandemic increasing demand for outdoor activities, the backcountry witnessed an unprecedented surge of newcomers. Many had worried these newbies would haphazardly enter the mountains, sparking an explosion of avalanche fatalities. But, in retrospect, it wasn't really the newbies who proved to be the biggest problem. As McCammon had found in his dataset back in the early 2000s, more often than not, it proved to be experienced backcountry adventurers who got themselves in the most trouble. You could call it the avalanche paradox.

The snow-covered backcountry is a difficult place for human psychology. Snowy slopes are not inherently scary for experienced skiers, and it may be hard for them to recognize danger and act accordingly. Adventures in the mountains can be idyllic and exhilarating, and psychological research suggests people may struggle to get into a precautionary mindset in such settings. Recreationists also spend a lot of money on equipment, drive hours to get to trailheads, and make arduous climbs to reach their objectives. When they're at the top, they may disregard obvious hazards and make the mistake of riding a fun-looking steep slope because of all the costs it took to get there. Social scientists call this the "sunk cost fallacy."

The backcountry is also what psychologist Robin Hogarth might call a "wicked learning environment," where people get poor feedback on their decisions. That's opposed to what he calls a "kind learning environment," where people get near-immediate feedback on their decisions. Conventional sports offer such feedback. For example, if you shoot a basketball a certain way, and it consistently doesn't go in, there's a good chance you'll learn to shoot differently. That's because you get immediate feedback on your shots. And, often, you'll have

Ian McCammon (center) developed two highly influential avalanche safety acronyms, FACETS and ALPTRUTh, providing skiers with an efficient way to make better decisions in the backcountry.

ORIGINAL PHOTO: Karl Birkeland.

a coach and teammates who can help you along the way.

But the backcountry is a place where you can ski the same slope 99 times and not get hurt—and maybe that's just because you've been very lucky. The repetition can lull you into overconfidence, where your brain goes on autopilot, using heuristic rules—like familiarity—instead of critically assessing potential dangers. But weather conditions can dramatically change—and a persistent weak layer of faceted snow or other avalanche dangers can form in the snowpack. And, on the 100th time you head down your favorite slope, *whumpf*, you're a goner.

Beyond heuristics leading people to peril, research from behavioral economist George Loewenstein suggests that adventurers in the backcountry disregard obvious hazards because of the role that emotions can play in their decision-making. Some people, particularly young men, find taking risks to be inherently exciting, which is likely another contributor to unnecessary deaths in the backcountry. It's also one that could be harder to combat.

McCammon's aim, however, is not to dictate which risks adventurers should or shouldn't take. Instead, he seeks to help them base whichever decisions they make on a clear-eyed assessment of danger. Decisions will vary depending on each person's appetite for risk. "My goal has been to give people the tools that

they need to objectively assess the hazard and make a risk-management-based decision," he says. "It's ultimately up to them."

To overcome all the psychological problems that people could encounter in the backcountry, Tremper says again and again in his textbook, "The system is the solution." Tremper says that paid backcountry professionals, like ski guides and heli-skiing outfits, have figured out really effective systems for navigating the hazards of the mountains. They rely on careful analysis of the snowpack. They have team meetings in the morning, running through checklists about conditions and doing premortem exercises. They identify specific areas where it's safe to travel and then stick to that terrain. They have alternative plans ready if on-the-ground conditions are worse than expected. In the evening, they debrief about their decision-making that day and assess how they can improve it in the future. Their rigorous systems explain, Tremper says, why backcountry professionals have remarkably low fatality rates despite their frequent outings in high-risk terrain.

But these are paid professionals with bosses and clients and bureaucracy and money on the line. A major challenge in the backcountry, Tremper says, is that most excursions are undertaken by non-professionals who must vet their decision-making themselves. The challenge, he says, is getting people to voluntarily adopt systems to keep them safe.

"When you're a professional operation—and people's paychecks depend on abiding by the rules—then you've got some leverage," Tremper says. "But how do you implement such a system in a peer setting? I think that's the holy grail of this whole human factors thing."

Before he retired, Tremper sought to improve how the Utah Avalanche Center and other avalanche centers communicate dangers to the public. "An avalanche forecaster in Colorado, Dale Atkins, told me this for years: 'We don't have an avalanche forecasting problem. We have a marketing problem.'" Tremper spent much of his career trying to solve this marketing problem. He, for example, created daily advisory reports that were easy—and even fun—to read. He used eye-catching graphics to communicate danger. He got the center to use social media and YouTube to educate the public about problems in the snowpack.

Tremper has long been concerned about the official warning systems that many avalanche centers use. In the United States and Canada, local advisory systems have adopted what's called "The North American Avalanche Danger Scale." It communicates dangers to the public with five levels: low, moderate, considerable, high, and extreme. Most accidents occur on days when centers warn that the danger is "considerable"—and Tremper has long suspected that one contributor to the problem is that the word "considerable" does not effectively communicate danger. "I hate that word," he says. "I wish I could wave a magic wand and change it—and I've sat on committees for years trying to get that done." He prefers a system adopted by many European countries, which communicates danger more simply with colors and numbers.

While there is still much room for improvement, avalanche institutions have made tremendous progress tackling the human factor. For example, the American Institute for Avalanche Research and Education, the main organization for educating American backcountry travelers, now embeds many of McCammon's ideas and analyses in its avalanche courses.

Interestingly enough, McCammon's FACETS framework has found resonance in realms outside of the backcountry. He's taught professionals like doctors, attorneys, and astronauts how heuristic traps can lead them into trouble. He says he gets them to think about bad decisions and mistakes they've made in the past. And then he has them run a "FACETS test," asking them to think about which heuristics potentially led them astray. Often, he says, they uncover patterns in their decision-making weaknesses—and he's hopeful that this will help them spot and override their defective decision-making rules going forward.

In 2016, the American Avalanche Association bestowed McCammon with their highest award. "It is impossible to quantify the number of people who have not perished in avalanches due to Ian's research and his impact on avalanche education and methodology," the presenter said. "However, what we can say is that Ian has effected a sea change in the way in which we talk not only about snow, but about ourselves."

People will, sadly, continue to make dumb decisions in the mountains that cost them their lives. But thanks to people like Ian McCammon—who took a tragedy and made it a call to arms—backcountry adventurers now have better tools and a more informed community working to nudge them towards safety. ∎

Greg Rosalsky is a reporter at NPR's Planet Money. He writes a weekly newsletter about economics and regularly contributes to the show's podcasts and NPR's radio programs. Prior to this, he was a producer at *Freakonomics Radio* and a freelance writer at various publications. He earned a master's degree at the Princeton School of Public and International Affairs, where he studied economics and public policy.

Group Conflict: Its Course and Possible Cure

By Muzafer Sherif

To highlight the parallels between summer camp activities and real-world conflict, Muzafer Sherif's summary of the three camp studies, published in *The Washington Post* in 1969, featured a photograph of a group of young boys playing in the water alongside a painting of soldiers fighting in the American Revolutionary War.

PART 5

Journey to Robbers Cave

"Although individuals fight from motives of lust, aggression and dominance, conflict between peoples and groups is seldom a bellicose outburst of naked passion. And although individuals fight, they do not wage war or exterminate a people. These are organized activities, requiring long-range goals and planning among persons dedicated to the designs of their group. They are conducted, as a rule, by the more able and steadfast in their fold."

"THE WORLD LEADERS SHOULD HEED the lesson of the experiment."

Muzafer Sherif did not mince words when he shared a summary of the camp studies with the public in 1969 within the pages of *The Washington Post*. But this was 15 years after the final camp, and it was one of only a small handful of articles authored by Sherif in the popular press.

When he did speak of the camps, Sherif merged the three in his summaries and focused primarily on the 1954 results—the only camp in which they reached the final stage and conflict was resolved. He also made clear how he interpreted the actions of the boys: the vandalism of the cabin of the opposing group was a "raid" while the collection of apples was the "stockpiling of ammunition." From Sherif's perspective, these were not merely summer camps but also a mirror for the rising tensions between nations.

The camp studies, or the 1954 camp to be exact, became the best-known demonstration of realistic group conflict theory—a model of intergroup conflict in social psychology. It may be the novelty of the approach alone that resulted in the popularity of the experiment; Sherif and his colleagues were not particularly active advocates. Aside from a hand-

ful of academic articles and presentations, the team only published the results of the 1954 Robbers Cave study initially as a technical report that was distributed privately to colleagues. The full book version was not published until 1961, and then with a small publisher at the University of Oklahoma. The study results would not see larger distribution until the text was republished in 1988.

In classic researcher style, Sherif took less interest in communicating the meaning of his research for the real-world to others and instead focused his time expanding on the lessons learned within the camp studies, investigating intergroup conflict—and group dynamics more generally—in new settings with expanded participant pools.

Experiments in Group Conflict

What are the conditions which lead to harmony or friction between groups of people? Here the question is approached by means of controlled situations in a boys' summer camp

by Muzafer Sherif

Conflict between groups—whether between boys' gangs, social classes, "races" or nations—has no simple cause, nor is mankind yet in sight of a cure. It is often rooted deep in personal, social, economic, religious and historical forces. Nevertheless it is possible to identify certain general factors which have a crucial influence on the attitude of any group toward others. Social scientists have long sought to bring these factors to light by studying what might be called the "natural history" of groups and group relations. Intergroup conflict and harmony is not a subject that lends itself easily to laboratory experiments. But in recent years there has been a beginning of attempts to investigate the problem under controlled yet lifelike conditions, and I shall report here the results of a program of experimental studies of groups which I started in 1948. Among the persons working with me were Marvin B. Sussman, Robert Huntington, O. J. Harvey, B. Jack White, William R. Hood and Carolyn W. Sherif. The experiments were conducted in 1949, 1953 and 1954; this article gives a composite of the findings.

We wanted to conduct our study with groups of the informal type, where group organization and attitudes would evolve naturally and spontaneously, without formal direction or external pressures. For this purpose we conceived that an isolated summer camp would make a good experimental setting, and that decision led us to choose as subjects boys about 11 or 12 years old, who would find camping natural and fascinating. Since our aim was to study the development of group relations among these boys under carefully controlled conditions, with as little interference as possible from personal neuroses, background influences or prior experiences, we selected normal boys of homogeneous background who did not know one another before they came to the camp.

They were picked by a long and thorough procedure. We interviewed each boy's family, teachers and school officials, studied his school and medical records, obtained his scores on personality tests and observed him in his classes and at play with his schoolmates. With all this information we were able to assure ourselves that the boys chosen were of like kind and background: all were healthy, socially well-adjusted, somewhat above average in intelligence and from stable, white, Protestant, middleclass homes.

None of the boys was aware that he was part of an experiment on group relations. The investigators appeared as a regular camp staff—camp directors, counselors and so on. The boys met one another for the first time in buses that

MEMBERS OF ONE GROUP of boys raid the bunkhouse of another group during the first experiment of the author and his associates, performed at a summer camp in Connecticut. The rivalry of the groups was intensified by the artificial separation of their goals.

2

Muzafer Sherif shared a summary of the three camp studies, complete with original photographs capturing the boys' activities, in *Scientific American* in 1956.

"The reason a special point is made of these apple ('ammunition') collecting activity is that these particular pictures represent their own unauthorized planned activity in hoarding apples for future raids which the camp authorities (counselors etc.) tried to stop."

Handwritten note from Muzafer Sherif paired with photographs used in presentations to explain how the research team interpreted the boys collecting apples to throw at the other group.

The reason a special point is made of these apple ("ammunition") collecting activity is that these particular pictures represent their own unauthorized planned activity in hoarding apples for future raids which the camp authorities (counselors etc.) tried to stop.

(↓)

I want to send this brief memorandum to tell you how much I enjoyed your lecture last night in the Business Administration Auditorium.

Of course, after listening to your description of the group tensions which developed in the controlled experiment in Connecticut in the homogeneous groups with identical religious background, etc., I came away with a heavy heart with respect to the world situation.

Those of us who are particularly interested in international law will follow closely your projected experiments with respect to relieving group tensions and inter-group conflicts. The analogy between our current program of stock-piling ammunition, guns, and other war essentials, and the barrel of apples which were gathered by the youngsters in your experiment serves as a reminder that grown men are just little boys after all.

Excerpt of a memo received by Muzafer Sherif following a lecture he gave in 1950 in which he drew attention to the analogy between armed conflict in the real world and the collection of apples by boys in the 1949 camp.

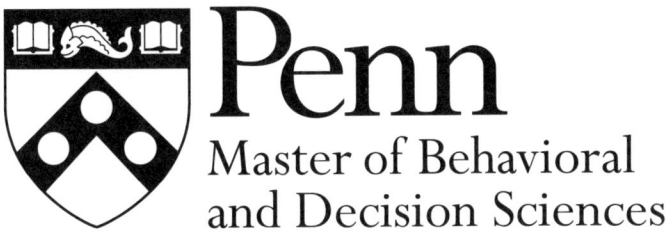

Penn's Master of Behavioral and Decision Sciences (MBDS) is informed by contemporary theories and research methods of behavioral economics, decision sciences, network analysis, and public policy.

Our program equips students with theoretical and practical tools to address a variety of real-life problems, putting you ahead of the curve in a growing field of study.

The interdisciplinary MBDS degree is rooted in the social sciences and prepares you to understand how individuals and groups make decisions, and how to affect those decisions. Our world-renowned faculty and researchers are also leading practitioners in their fields. With their expertise, you are guided to apply what you learn to real-life problems in areas such as social and public policy, law, education, business, and medicine.

Visit us at **upenn.edu/MBDS**
Find us on Facebook: **facebook.com/PennMBDS**

A Cognitive Labor of Love

By Allison Daminger

My partner, E., is responsible for taking the trash out to the curb on Sunday evenings. But on a recent Monday as I was sitting down to work, I noticed that the garbage bin next to my desk hadn't yet been emptied. I spent a good five minutes dithering over what to do next. My thoughts went something like this:

If I remind him to do it, he might expect me to remind him in the future. And if he expects a reminder, then I'll have to add "trash day" to the long list of tasks already swimming through my brain and crowding out more important stuff. Then again, if I forgot, I'd probably appreciate a gentle reminder. Everybody slips up from time to time. But ugh, this is so gendered! Why am I the one thinking about this?! If he can't remember to take out the trash, how will he remember to pick up our future children from daycare?!

This may seem like an extreme reaction to an objectively unimportant incident. But before you judge me too harshly, consider some background: I'm a sociologist who studies the division of household labor. I focus on the cognitive aspects of that labor, which you can think of as project management for the household. Who finds a plumber to fix the leaky faucet? Who notices that a child has outgrown her shoes? Who remembers that it's trash day?

In most of the different-sex couples I've spoken with (75 and counting!), the answer is usually that the female partner does it. Women do more cognitive labor overall, and a *lot* more of the work of anticipating, remembering, tracking, and monitoring. Men are often involved in making important decisions for the household. But it's typically women who initiate the decision-making process and, later, who follow up to make sure everything went as planned.

When I began this research, I was single and mostly motivated by curiosity about the weird stuff I saw coupled people doing. Why were my feminist friends doing all the wedding planning? Why did the moms I spoke with know *way* more about their children's needs than the dads did, even though they described themselves as equal partners?

After conducting dozens of interviews, reading hundreds of academic papers, and thinking about these questions for untold hours, I considered myself an expert on household labor. I offered advice to couples looking to share their cognitive workload more equitably. Above all, I was confident that my extensive knowledge would keep me from falling into the gendered patterns I observed among my research subjects. Instead, I planned to have an equitable partnership. Not necessarily one where every chore was split 50/50, but one where my hypothetical partner and I divided up the load thoughtfully, rather than unwittingly use gender as a heuristic for assigning responsibilities.

And then I met E., and the issues I was accustomed to documenting and diagnosing as an observer became my everyday life. If I initiated a conversation about weekend plans and coordinated meetups with friends, I worried about becoming the default social coordinator (a typical female responsibility). When he offered to pay for dates, I was torn between gratitude and guilt. My graduate student stipend was minimal compared to his salary, but

I also hated to replicate the trope of the male provider and the female dependent on his financial support.

Hence my uncertainty over what to do on trash day. When you're an expert on household labor, a garbage can is never *just* a garbage can.

Much to my disappointment, I soon realized that knowledge and good intentions would not be enough to buck the norm and help us forge an equitable relationship. Figuring out when to just accept that, for whatever reason, I enjoy organizing dinner parties and he does not, and when to push for a less traditionally gendered arrangement, was a decision my research could not make for me.

Also working against us were the expectations of others (parents, grandparents, family friends, and random strangers) who usually mean well but sometimes find E.'s and my choices strange, like when we got engaged—without a ring.

We had discussed the engagement beforehand and decided that the asymmetry of a diamond on my finger and nothing on his set the wrong precedent for the egalitarian marriage we hoped to build. I felt good about our decision but second-guessed myself as soon as that decision became public knowledge. Friends asked for ring pictures, and I had none to offer. My father sent me links to jewelry websites in hopes I would change my mind. Every single engagement card we received had a giant rock on the front. I realized that our personal choice was something we would have to explain to others—and that many would not understand.

Whereas my research is characterized by clarity and logic, my life is far messier. Fortunately, over time E. and I have come up with strategies for managing the mess. Though my academic knowledge failed to magically protect me from the challenges of pursuing an egalitarian relationship in a gendered world, it *has* helped me design systems and habits that make it a little easier for us to swim upstream.

When E. and I moved in together, for instance, one of the first things we did after unpacking the boxes was divvy up responsibility for physical and cognitive housework. We enumerated all the shared tasks, agreed on standards for their completion, and recorded each person's duties in a spreadsheet. A decidedly unsexy solution. But a solution.

Parts of the division we came up with are traditional: I do more of the cooking and laundry, for instance, and E. takes out the trash and cares for the car. I was tempted to volunteer for all the "male" tasks, just to counter the stereotypes. Then I remembered that I *hate* dealing with the trash cans and dread visits to the mechanic. Ultimately, we decided that ensuring our overall workloads are equal was more important to us than bucking traditions just to be contrary.

Especially in the early days, relationships are supposed to be made of spontaneity and romance, not routines and spreadsheets. The excitement of finding The One is supposed to crowd out prosaic concerns about who remembered to take out the trash. But spontaneity and romance provide little protection against the social forces that steer most different-sex couples down gender-traditional pathways. We, at least, need guardrails in place that remind us to align our actions with our values.

In the process of designing those guardrails, I've noticed parallels between the work of being a good social scientist and being a good partner. To succeed in research, one has to be willing to venture into the unknown, test things, fail, and most importantly bounce back from that failure again and again. To succeed in a new relationship, one must also learn to tolerate uncertainty, be willing to experiment and change, and commit to trying again when those experiments flop.

One more overlap: rigorous science and egalitarian partnership both tend to involve spreadsheets. When E. and I sat down to plan our wedding, you'd better believe our first steps were deciding on a shared vision, identifying the nonnegotiables we wouldn't be talked out of, and figuring out who would be responsible for which pieces of the process. We recorded those decisions in a spreadsheet, of course. ∎

Allison Daminger is a Ph.D. candidate in sociology and social policy at Harvard University and a fellow at the Radcliffe Institute for Advanced Study. Her research focuses on how and why gender continues to shape individuals' experiences at home and at work, even as support for gender-egalitarianism keeps growing.

Busara Center for Behavioral Economics is proud to be a supporting partner of *Behavioral Scientist*.

What defines Busara? Context.

It's our dedication to context that has rooted us deeply in the Global South. Whether from our headquarters in Kenya to offices in Nigeria, India, Tanzania, and Uganda, or projects in 25+ countries, we're committed to understanding the nuance of behavioral science where it's needed most.

From our team's diverse lived experience and expertise, to academic partnerships and publications, Busara bridges the gap between scientific and applied work. Our Lab-in-a-Box (conversion of labs to different countries and contexts) and KITE (remote data collection) platforms ensure that time, space, or geography are not limitations on our research.

We can't do it alone! Our mission is to work with researchers and organizations to advance and apply behavioral science in pursuit of poverty alleviation, and we mean it. Partner with us to understand human behaviors and design solutions to scale. Or join our diverse team hailing from 15+ countries to carry out this rigorous, practical, and impactful work.

Learn more at **busaracenter.org**
Find us on Twitter: **@busaracenter**

The Brain—Is Wider than the Sky

By Emily Dickinson

The Brain—is wider than the Sky—
For—put them side by side—
The one the other will contain
With ease—and you—beside—

The Brain is deeper than the sea—
For—hold them—Blue to Blue—
The one the other will absorb—
As sponges—Buckets—do—

The Brain is just the weight of God—
For—Heft them—Pound for Pound—
And they will differ—if they do—
As Syllable from Sound—

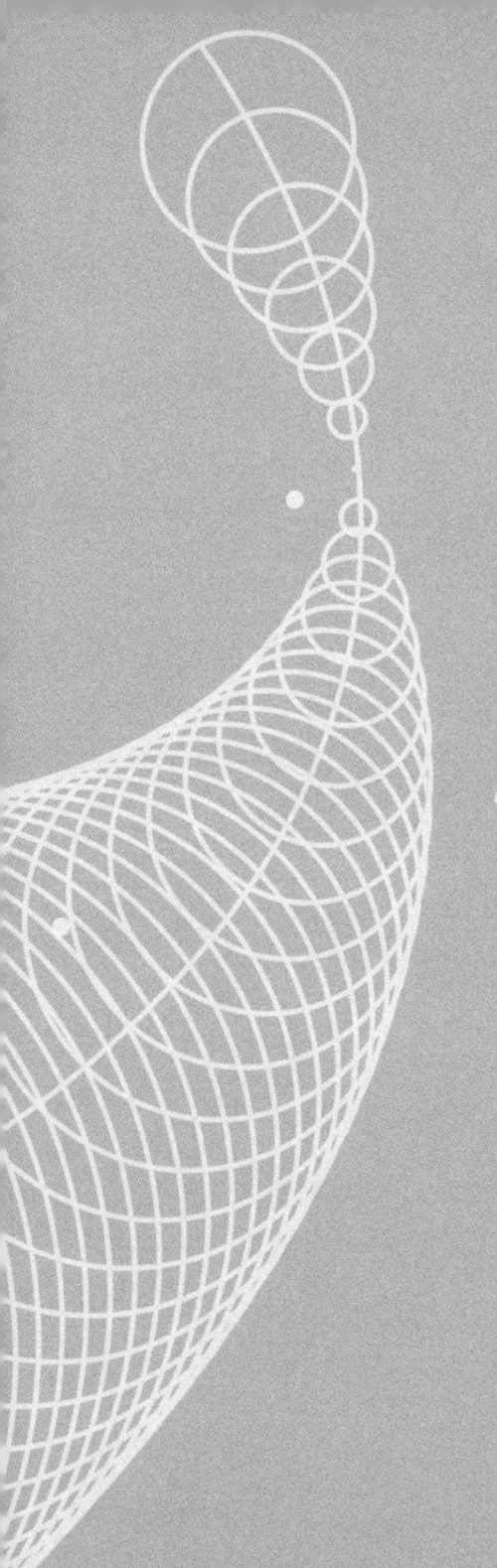

CHAPTER 6

Reflections

*"Man will become better when you show
him what he is like."*

—ANTON CHEKHOV

*"Beware of the man who works hard to
learn something, learns it, and finds
himself no wiser than before."*

—KURT VONNEGUT

Psychologists Go to War

By John Greenwood

A little over a century ago, on April 6, 1917, the United States entered World War I by declaring war on Germany. When American psychologists heard the news, they dispatched Robert M. Yerkes, then president of the American Psychological Association (APA), to Canada to confer with Carl C. Brigham of the Canadian Military Hospitals Commission to learn about the contributions that Canadian psychologists were already making to the war effort.

Yerkes was a comparative psychologist at Harvard University, where he had spent much of his career investigating the mental and behavioral processes of non-human animals, from invertebrates to reptiles, amphibians, and mice. In 1913, his work broadened to understanding the causes of and potential remedies for mental illness, when he was appointed as consulting psychologist at Boston Psychopathic Hospital. It was there that he developed an interest in the study of intelligence.

On his return to the United States, Yerkes pressed the APA to set up a dozen committees to explore the useful roles that psychologists might play in the war, ranging from the study of acoustic problems to improving recreational facilities for soldiers. Only two of these committees made any significant contribution. One was Yerkes's Committee on Methods of Psychological Examination for Recruits, which included Henry Goddard and Lewis Terman, two pioneers of intelligence testing in the United States.

The committee had originally planned to implement a variety of tests for recruits, such as tests of intelligence, memory, and suggestibility. They eventually restricted themselves to intelligence testing, with the aim of "segregating and eliminating the mentally incompetent,"—or "feeblemind-ed," in the parlance of the day—from the military.

Their work accomplished its primary aim, initiating the largest program of psychological testing that had been attempted to that date. But, unforeseen, it also fueled two movements that had been developing since the turn of the century: the call for immigration quotas and the sterilization of the so called feebleminded.

Intelligence testing in the Army

I n May 1917, realizing that it would be impractical to test intelligence one recruit at a time, Yerkes's committee spent two weeks developing tests that could be administered in groups and conducting trials of these tests at educational institutions and Army bases. Working through the National Research Council, Yerkes proposed group intelligence testing to the Army, which created the Division of Psychology under the Surgeon General. When Yerkes's plan for the mass intelligence testing of Army recruits, dubbed the Army Testing Project, was approved, he commissioned a team of 400 Army personnel to administer group intelligence tests to all Army recruits.

The intelligence tests included the Alpha written test for literate soldiers and the Beta pictorial test for those who could not read English. On the Alpha test were items like arithmetic word problems, analogy completion tests, and questions assessing general knowledge. The Beta test asked recruits to do things like identify what was wrong or missing from a set of pictures.

By the end of the war, close to 2 million soldiers had been tested. On the basis of the test results, about 8,000 men were recommended for immediate discharge on grounds of mental incompetence, and another 19,000 were assigned to labor and noncombat battalions.

Psychologists who participated in the Army Testing Project felt they had made a valuable, practical contribution, and found their work an exhilarating contrast to normal academic life. (Yerkes himself regretted that the war did not last longer.) Publications such as *Harper's Magazine* and *The New York Times* lauded their achievement. However, the Army itself was less than enthusiastic, and discontinued the program shortly after the war ended. (In contrast, the Army judged the other major psychological war committee a great success. Walter Dill Scott's Committee on the Classification of Personnel in the Army developed scales for officer selection, and in 1918 Scott was awarded the Distinguished Service Medal.)

Though it was short-lived as part of military efforts, the Army Testing Project had significant consequences in the social sphere.

Fears of a creeping "feeblemindedness"

One of the striking findings of the Army Testing Project was that around half of the Army recruits tested at or below the level of "moron." The term *moron* had been introduced by Henry Goddard to classify adults with the mental age of a child between 10 and 12. Individuals judged to have a mental age between 4 and 10 years were classified as low-grade, medium-grade, or high-grade "imbeciles"; those with a mental age of 3 or under were classified as "idiots."

First Company of Commissioned Psychologists, School for Military Psychology, Camp Greenleaf. Robert M. Yerkes inset bottom right.

SOURCE: Yerkes, 1921.

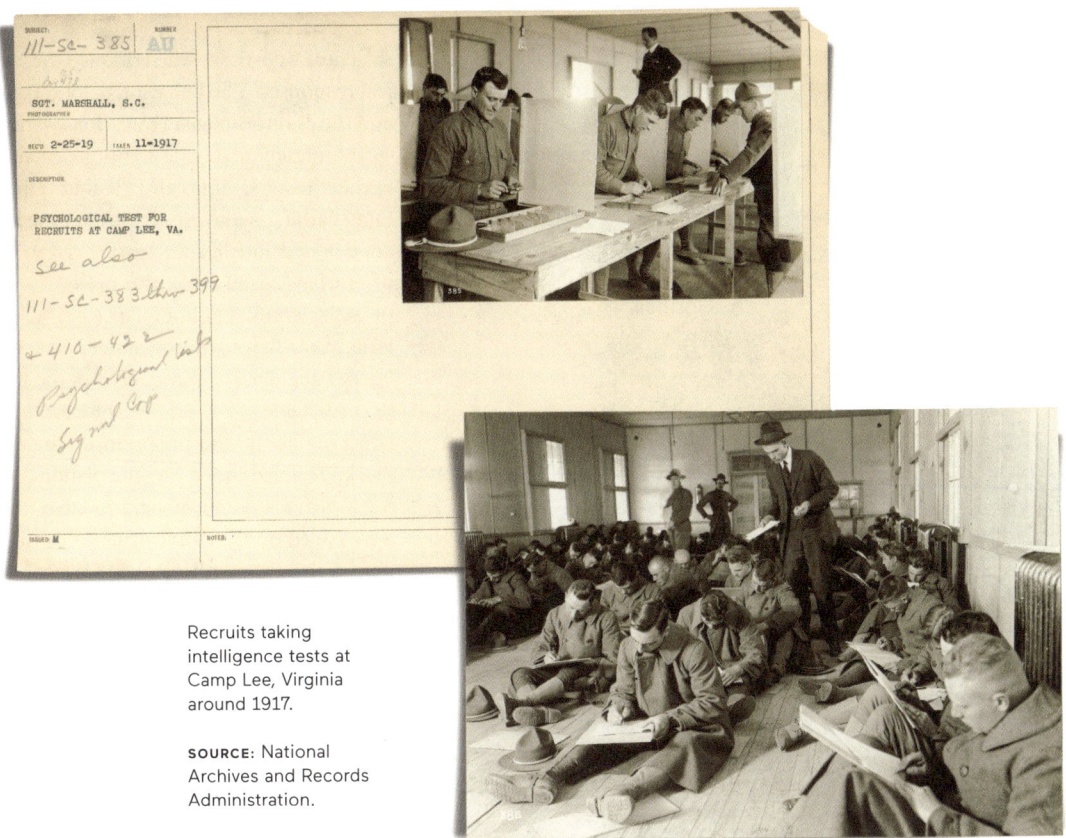

Recruits taking intelligence tests at Camp Lee, Virginia around 1917.

SOURCE: National Archives and Records Administration.

These classifications were based on Goddard's translations of the 1908 and 1909 Binet-Simon intelligence scale, which Terman revised in 1916. Terman's revision, which was later known as the Stanford-Binet test (after Terman became professor of psychology at Stanford University), became the standard American intelligence test.

In the first decade of the twentieth century, French psychologists Alfred Binet and Théodore Simon had introduced a scale for measuring a child's intelligence. The scale comprises 54 tests. These were arranged according to appropriate age levels between 3 and 13 years old, calibrated so the average 9-year-old would score at level 9. Binet and Simon used the term "mental level" rather than the later term "mental age" because they believed their scale was a useful means of identifying children in need of remedial education (for whom they devised special educational programs) rather than as a fixed measure of intelligence. However, Goddard and Terman treated the Binet-Simon tests as though they measured genetically determined intelligence.

The disconcerting findings of the Army Testing Project led Yerkes to conclude that "feeble-mindedness ... is of much greater frequency than had previously been supposed" and caused a moral panic among psychologists, politicians, and the public at large. A number of works that were both alarmist and racist publicized the supposedly dire consequences of allowing immigrants from eastern and southern Europe to displace (and contaminate) the original Nordic (northern and western European) "stock." For example, Carl Brigham, who had advised Yerkes on the Canadian war effort and later helped develop the Alpha intelligence test, claimed in his 1923 book *A Study of American Intelligence* that the average intelligence of recent immigrants was less than that of native-born Americans. The average intelligence of Americans, he argued, had been declining since 1900.

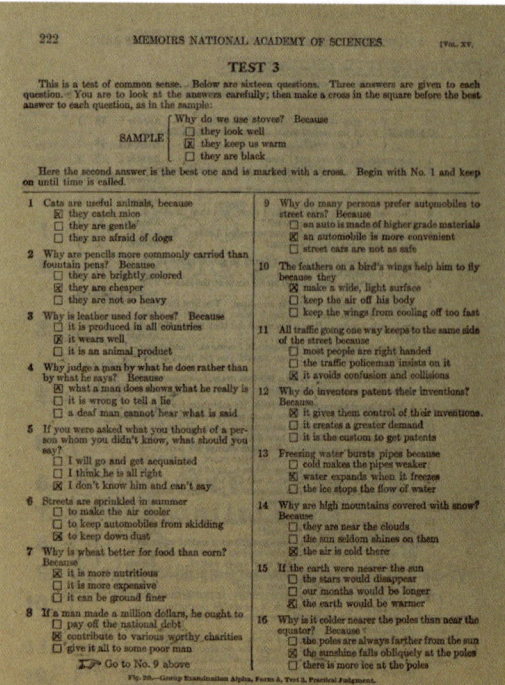

Examples of the Alpha and Beta intelligence tests given to recruits.

SOURCE:
Yerkes, 1921.

National Archives and Records Administration. Photographs of American Military Activities, ca. 1918 - ca. 1981.

Yerkes, R. M. (Ed.). (1921). Psychological examining in the United States army. *Memoirs of the National Academy of Sciences* (Vol. 15). Washington, DC: Government Printing Office.

There were those who critiqued these hysterical responses. The behaviorist John B. Watson and the anthropologist Franz Boas were critical of the hereditarian presumptions of the intelligence testers. Journalist Walter Lippmann, in a scathing series of articles in *New Republic,* condemned intelligence testing as an "engine of cruelty" based upon the pretentious abuse of the scientific method. Their efforts were to little avail. Before the members of Congress, Harry Laughlin, superintendent of the Eugenics Records Office at Cold Stream Harbor, voiced concerns about the pollution of the national stock. This led in 1924 to the National Origins Act, which restricted immigration to quotas that were based on the 1890 census—a census taken before the twentieth century wave of eastern and southern European immigration.

State-sanctioned eugenics

Several years earlier, fears about degeneracy in the general population had led Charles Davenport, author of *Eugenics: The Science of Human Improvement by Better Breeding*, to found in 1910 the Eugenics Records Office at Cold Stream Harbor, New York, an office dedicated to research on the inheritance of psychological traits, including intelligence and feeblemindedness. The British hereditarian Francis Galton had previously coined the term *eugenics* (from the Greek for "well-born") to describe his suggested program for improving the national stock. Galton, like many of his contemporaries, had recognized that one of the implications of his half-cousin Charles Darwin's theory of evolution was that human progress was not inevitable: humankind, if left to its own devices, was just as likely to degenerate as to progress. This concern was seemingly confirmed by rising crime, alcoholism, tuberculosis, and feeblemindedness among the Victorian lower classes.

Galton originally recommended programs of positive eugenics. In these programs, the "highly-gifted" (assessed via Galton's own measures of human intelligence) should be encouraged through generous financial government incentives to breed and to breed often. However, the Boer War, in South Africa, shifted Galton's view. The war lasted from 1899 to 1902, far from the quick and decisive victory that many expected when the British Empire was pitched against a nation of farmers. Galton and his protégé Karl Pearson fretted that reduced levels of "national efficiency" were in fact a threat to national survival. They suggested programs of negative eugenics, through which the state would institutionalize and sterilize those deemed mentally defective.

In 1914, before working on the Army Testing Project, Yerkes and Goddard had served on the Committee to Study and to Report on the Best Practical Means of Cutting Off the Defective Germ-Plasm in the American Population, a research committee that had been commissioned by the American Breeders Association. After considering the options of life segregation (compulsory institutionalization), restrictive marriage laws, eugenic education (to encourage "educable defectives" to voluntarily decline to propagate their kind), general environmental betterment (to improve social conditions), and euthanasia, they recommended segregation and sterilization as the "most feasible and effective in cutting off from the human population the supply of defectives."

State legislatures quickly adopted their recommendation. By 1930, around 30 states had sterilization laws on their books, and within five years approximately 35,000 individuals had been sterilized. Harry Laughlin, who had promoted the National Origins Act in Congress, published in 1922 a Model Eugenical Sterilization Law, which became the template for most state laws. The law targeted those persons "who, because of degenerate or defective hereditary qualities, are potential parents of socially inadequate offspring," and its stated aim was to "prevent certain degenerate human stock from reproducing its kind."

Once again there was opposition, but again it came to naught. In 1927 the Supreme Court heard the case of *Buck* v. *Bell*. At question was the right of the State of Virginia to sterilize Carrie Buck, who along with her mother and illegitimate daughter, Vivian, had been classified as feebleminded. (Vivian's illegitimacy was taken as evidence of Carrie's feeblemindedness; in fact, Carrie had been raped by a nephew of the foster parents who committed her.) The Supreme Court ruled in favor of the State of Virginia, and Carrie Buck was sterilized. Justice Oliver Wendell Holmes Jr., writing in favor of the majority, claimed:

It is better for all the world, if instead of waiting to execute degenerate offspring for crime, or to let them starve for their imbecility, society can prevent those who are manifestly unfit from continuing their kind.... Three generations of imbeciles are enough.

This movement had international appeal. Laughlin's Model Eugenical Sterilization Law also formed the legal basis of Germany's 1933 Law for the Prevention of Genetically Diseased Offspring, which sanctioned the sterilization of 350,000 "hereditarily diseased" persons, including anyone deemed mentally deficient, schizophrenic, manic-depressive, or epileptic, as well as anyone who happened to be congenitally blind, deaf, or severely "deformed."

Enthusiasm for the sterilization of the feebleminded waned in the United States after Nazi Germany extended eugenic programs to wholesale extermination programs. By the 1930s many psychologists had recanted their earlier positions. Carl Brigham, for one, dismissed his earlier claims about inheritance and degeneracy as "without foundation." Nonetheless, the practice continued in the United States into the 1960s, by which time around 65,000 individuals had been sterilized. The last sterilization law was removed only in 1981.

The Army Testing Project had one other consequence of social significance. After the war, Carl Brigham joined the psychology faculty at Princeton University, where in 1925 he devised a college admissions test based upon the Army Alpha test, which he had helped to create. The following year, Brigham developed his test into the Scholastic Achievement Test (SAT) for the College Board. Once again, he had a change of heart, later condemning the use of the SAT and opposing the creation of the Educational Testing Service. By then, of course, that train had long since left the station. ■

John Greenwood is professor in philosophy and psychology at the City University of New York Graduate Center. His primary research is in the history and philosophy of social and psychological science. He is the author of *The Disappearance of the Social in American Social Psychology* and *A Conceptual History of Psychology: Exploring the Tangled Web*.

PART 6

Journey to Robbers Cave

SUMMER CAMP was not the final scene of Muzafer and Carolyn Wood Sherif's research into group behavior. They brought their observational work to other settings, diversifying their participant groups in terms of age, gender, and race. While intergroup conflict remained core to their collaborative work program, the Sherifs expanded their focus to include other elements of a group's dynamics, like conformity to and deviation from group norms, and the hierarchy of relationships among members.

In 1966, the Sherifs moved from Oklahoma, where they had been since 1949, to Pennsylvania State University. Muzafer took his interdisciplinary methods into the sociology department, while Carolyn increasingly shifted her research toward the psychology of gender, becoming a founding member of the Society for the Psychology of Women (Division 35 of the American Psychological Association).

Throughout their careers, Muzafer and Carolyn wrote extensively about their research on groups, jointly publishing nine books in addition to their own respective works. But their names would become inextricably entwined with the 1954 Robbers Cave camp, their larger research program overshadowed. And as psychologists have looked back on psychology's classic studies, the Sherifs' legacy has found itself at the center of renewed controversy.

YOUTH SURVEY

The University of Oklahoma

You have probably heard about surveys or polls of people's ideas. This is a survey of young people. It is not like an examination. On most questions, the "right" answer is what fits you, what you really feel or think. Your answers will be read only by people who do not know you and will not be read by your friends, parents or teachers.

You can help a great deal if you will answer every question just as you think, even if you are not sure.

PART I

Here are some sentences with words left out. You are to fill in the words to complete the sentence so that it fits you.

FOR EXAMPLE:

1. I live (WHERE?)_____in the state of_____.
   (YOU PUT WHERE YOU LIVE ON THE FIRST BLANK AND YOUR STATE IN THE SECOND.)

2. I have _____ brothers and _____ sisters.

3. When I am through with my education at schools, the kind of work and the job I want is _____.
   (PLEASE PUT DOWN THE KIND OF WORK OR OCCUPATION YOU WANT. IF YOU HONESTLY DON'T HAVE ANY IDEA, PLEASE SAY SO.)

4. A person my age needs $_____ spending money a week.

5. A person my age should be able to go to the movies_____ times a week.

6. A person should have at least _____(minutes or hours) a day to do just what he or she wants to do.

7. The farthest I have ever traveled in this state was to _____ which is about _____ miles away from where I live.

8. The longest trip outside of this state I ever made was to _____
   (PLACE
   _____, which is about _____ miles away from here.
   STATE)

9. If a person wants to earn a living, he has to work at least_____ hours a day.

Survey and demographic data collected by the Sherifs as part of their continued research into groups following the camp studies.

Map of Norman, OK showing the variation in monthly housing rental rates. It was created by Sherif during the development of a 1958 study of adolescent group behavior in a city experiencing high degrees of transition.

It is better to stick to one job even if it gets dull (CHOOSE ONE) Yes X No

Going to school is dull because _you do the same thing every day_

Going to school is fun because _you learn things you didn't previously know and see people_

Working on a job is dull because _you do the same work all the time_

Working on a job is fun because _you get paid and meet people_

Survey data collected by the Sherifs as part of their continued research into groups following the camp studies.

Preface   *program in social psychology*

For close to twenty years a substantial part of our research and writing has been devoted to the vital problem area of intergroup relations. The problem area of intergroup relations embraces all the major topics of social psychology, and , even, for that matter, of all psychology — perception, learning, (motivation (aggression, cooperation), emotion, categorizing, stereotyping, effects of group membership. (cover a vast territory), though there psychological topics are , the study of intergroup relations

Handwritten draft of a preface prepared by Muzafer Sherif that highlights his vision concerning the importance of intergroup relations to other areas in psychology. "For close to twenty years a substantial part of our research and writing [program in social psychology] has been devoted to the vital problem area of intergroup relations. The problem area of intergroup relations embraces all the major topics of social psychology, even, for that matter of all psychology—perception, learning, motivation (aggression, cooperation), emotion, categorizing, stereotyping, effects of group membership. Through these psychological topics [cover vast territory], the study of intergroup relations …"

Principles for the Application of Human Intelligence

By Jason Collins

Recognition of the powerful pattern matching ability of humans is growing. As a result, humans are increasingly being deployed to make decisions that affect the well-being of other humans. We are starting to see the use of human decision makers in courts, in university admissions offices, in loan application departments, and in recruitment. Soon humans will be the primary gateway to many core services.

The use of humans undoubtedly comes with benefits relative to the data-derived algorithms that we have used in the past. The human ability to spot anomalies that are missed by our rigid algorithms is unparalleled. A human decision maker also allows us to hold someone directly accountable for the decisions.

However, the replacement of algorithms with a powerful technology in the form of the human brain is not without risks. Before humans become the standard way we make decisions, we need to consider the risks and ensure the implementation of human decision-making systems does not cause widespread harm. To this end, we need to develop principles for the application of human intelligence to decision-making.

Below I suggest four draft principles that we should apply to the use of human decision makers and describe how humans often fall short of meeting them. These principles are not complete but are designed to open to a conversation about how human decision-making can be deployed to greatest benefit. We need to do this before they become the default method of making decisions.

Avoid creating bias

Humans are biased decision makers, in more senses than one.

First, humans predictably and routinely deviate from many of the established rules of probability and logic. Humans have been shown to assign higher probabilities to specific events than the larger set of events for which they are also a part. Humans often neglect the base rate occurrence of an event, focusing on the idiosyncratic features of the particular case in front of them in determining its probability.

Undoubtedly, some of what we call biases come from a misunderstanding of the objectives of the decision maker. "Biased" decision rules may also be more likely to deliver good outcomes in an uncertain environment. But we now have ample evidence that people in some of our most important decision-making environments are systematically erring. For instance, judges and loan applications officers exhibit the gambler's fallacy. Doctors can be poor Bayesians when information is presented in unintuitive ways.

Second, humans demonstrate considerable bias against outgroups. They often output different decisions based on the sex, age, or race of the subject of the decision, despite those factors not being relevant to the decision.

While algorithms have certainly been demonstrated to be biased in some circumstances, due to both the data from which they were developed and the biases of the analyst developing them, the bias of these algorithms has typically been less severe. Further, the potential to systematically audit algorithms and implement improvements has steadily seen a reduction in their level of bias.

Various techniques have been developed to reduce human bias. Unfortunately, these techniques have limited demonstrated success at scale and may even backfire. Until these human debiasing techniques reach the efficiency of our regular auditing, review, and modification of algorithms, we should not implement these human decision systems.

Transparency and interpretability

Human minds are black boxes. While humans create the impression of transparency through the verbal and written explanations that they offer, there is strong evidence that these explanations cannot be trusted to provide the true basis for the decision.

One piece of evidence comes from Michael Gazzaniga's research into people with split brains. Some patients with severe epilepsy have the corpus callosum (which joins the two hemispheres of the brain) surgically severed, effectively resulting in two independent hemispheres.

Gazzaniga showed images to split brain patients. For patient P. S., he placed a chicken claw in the right visual field, which projects to the left hemisphere. He placed a snowy scene on the left, projecting to the right hemisphere. He then asked P. S. to point to one of an array of images and asked which matched the pictures P. S. had seen. P. S.'s right hand, linked to the left hemisphere, pointed to a chicken. The left hand, linked to the right hemisphere, pointed to a shovel. Why did P. S. point to the shovel? Here P. S.'s left hemisphere, where language capabilities typically sit, took over. "Oh, that's simple. The chicken claw goes with the chicken, and you need a shovel to clean out the chicken shed."

The mind is a great improviser. Or to put it more bluntly, in the absence of knowledge, the left hemisphere simply made the reason up.

The lack of transparency of the human mind is also apparent from broader experiments on how we reason. Typically, intuitions come first, reasons later. For instance, when hypnotized to feel a flash of disgust when reading arbitrary words, subjects later made up absurd reasons to justify judgments they had made on the basis of implanted words. Our gut feelings are integral to how we decide, yet the sources of these feelings are not observable or reliably reported.

Transparency is one of the most difficult principles to solve. We can never have access to the full training data that the human has been exposed to during their development. Absent this training data, we lack an understanding of the patterns that a particular human decision maker is likely to spot. Even if we can observe the full neural network that comprises the human

Before humans become the standard way we make decisions, we need to consider the risks and ensure the implementation of human decision-making systems does not cause widespread harm.

brain, we have no present ability to extract reasons from this observation.

Conversely, the algorithms we have chosen to implement in the past are clearer to understand. While some classes of algorithms, such as our deep neural nets, present difficulties in their interpretation, we have started to see the development of interpretative technologies. But more importantly, the simple algorithms we do tend to use still give us some great results while maintaining interpretability and transparency.

Consistency

Humans are noisy decision makers. Two different humans confronted with the same decision will often come to a different conclusion. The same human confronted with a decision on different occasions will also often decide inconsistently.

As examples of the size of this variation, software programmers differed by a median of 71 percent in the estimates for the time to complete the same project. Pathologists assessing biopsy results had a correlation of only 0.63 with their own judgment of severity when shown the same case twice (the same answer each time would result in a correlation of 1).

We are starting to use human decision makers in many domains where we should have consistent decisions. Gross differences in outcome are based on little more than the luck of the draw. And this burden does not fall equally. Those who are more sophisticated are able to exploit this inconsistency.

Conversely, provided we correctly measure and code the inputs, algorithms provide the same decision every time. Those subject to the decision are not going to be at the whim of how much sleep the decision maker had the night before, the order of their application in the queue, or the time of day (factors which the black box human mind does not include in the explanation of why they made the decision).

Standards of scientific excellence

Human decision makers are often poor substitutes for the primary purpose for which they are implemented. That is, they are typically outperformed by algorithms in decision-making quality. Today, as companies ride the zeitgeist and appoint their first Chief Human Officers, the human underperformance is often forgotten or ignored, with some classic stories of human success often overshadowing the more mundane lack of performance. In fact, it is difficult to find domains where human decision makers are clearly the superior option.

Stories of hybrid decision-making, in which humans work with algorithms, are common. They are often provided as a reason why we should include humans in the loop. Yet despite the stories about successful human-algorithm teams, the typical case results in degraded performance relative to the algorithm alone. To develop successful teams involving humans, we need much more work on how to get the humans to effectively work with the algorithms and avoid interposing their judgment too often.

Shaping the future of human decision makers

These principles are only the start of the discussion we need to have about the use of human decision makers. Before we deploy, we need to accept the basic evidence of the harm they cause in many situations, and their low accuracy, transparency, and consistency relative to algorithms.

We also need to continue building our evidence base. We should be systematically reviewing the quality of human decisions where they are made, measuring performance, and comparing those measures against our algorithmic benchmarks. Humans may be a powerful technology with great potential. But until we have developed human decision-making systems that comply with some basic principles, we risk substantial harm. ■

Jason Collins is an economist and behavioral scientist, consulting across government and the private sector. He cofounded and led PwC Australia's behavioral economics practice, was data science lead with an Australian regulator, has worked as a policy adviser with the Australian Treasury, and was a lawyer in private practice. He has a Ph.D. bridging economics and evolutionary biology from the University of Western Australia.

THE
BEHAVIOURAL
ARCHITECTS

A multi award-winning global insights and strategy agency specializing in applying behavioral science to real-world challenges.

Behavioral science powers a deeper understanding of behavior. For over ten years, The Behavioural Architects has pioneered the application of behavioral science alongside qualitative and quantitative research methods. Our work enables our clients to get closer to the true drivers of decision-making. Working with hundreds of the world's leading companies and organizations across both the public and private sector, we pride ourselves on our ability to both understand behavior and provide actionable strategies to change it.

The Behavioural Architects. Turning behavioral science into action.

London, Oxford, New York, Sydney, Melbourne, Shanghai

Learn more at **thebearchitects.com**
Find us on LinkedIn: **The Behavioural Architects**
Find us on Twitter: **@thebearchitects**

Goop Happens

By Traci Mann

I woke up one morning to an email from my aunt with the subject line "Are You OK?" and the message "I hate that they are doing this to you. I'm here if you want to talk." A similarly supportive and outraged email from my brother was further down in my inbox. I was wide awake now. What was this mysterious "they" doing, and why were my relatives so concerned about me? Clicking on the links in their emails sent me to a handful of blogs and news articles all referring to an irresponsible scientist who was recommending that people diet to the lowest weight they could achieve without dying.

As a psychologist who has spent nearly 25 years urging people not to diet, I was disgusted that anyone would recommend such an extreme goal. According to the articles, the person recommending this nonsense was University of Minnesota professor of psychology Traci Mann. Which was surprising, because I am University of Minnesota professor of psychology Traci Mann. And I would never suggest such a thing. Why were all these articles saying that I did? After poking around a bit, I had my answer: I did say those things. Repeatedly.

The offending article that started the cascade of hostility was a Q&A I had done for Goop.com. Yep, that Goop: Gwyneth Paltrow's lifestyle website, infamous for selling obscenely expensive luxury items and dispensing questionable health and diet advice. I participated in the Q&A for Goop specifically because I wanted to reach that audience of extreme dieters with my message to stop dieting and focus on health instead.

But this was not a case of Goop misquoting me. In fact, I had been so concerned about them misquoting me that I had only agreed to do the Q&A if I could provide written responses to their questions and approve the final version. It was also not the case that I had chosen my words carelessly, inadvertently saying the opposite of what I meant. I used three words that I routinely used in talks, and that I had thought about for a long time before selecting for frequent repetition in my book on dieting. I thought they helped simplify a complex idea.

I was horrified that morning to realize that my three carefully chosen words could be mistaken for terrible diet advice if you plucked them out of the sentences they were in. I urged people to strive for their "leanest livable weight." It looked like I was recommending that people diet until their weight was so low they could just barely cling to life. Did I mean that? Absolutely not. If anything, I meant close to the opposite. I was trying to recommend a sensible middle ground between the overly broad recommendation for practically everybody to go on calorie-restricting weight-loss diets and the overly lax suggestion that everyone should entirely ignore their weight and eat anything they wanted, in any quantity, at any time.

The middle ground I try to stake out is based on the idea that everyone has a set range of weights that their body will defend through multiple biomechanisms, including, among others, changes to metabolism and levels of satiety hormones. If your weight goes too far below that set range, those mechanisms kick in, and successfully maintaining that weight therefore requires an increasingly restrictive diet, vigilant monitoring of every bite, and a single-minded focus on that one goal. Most dieters find that their quality of life takes a severe hit when they try to live this way, and most regain the lost weight (often with additional weight on top of it) over time anyway, making the whole miserable experience counterproductive.

My recommendation was (and is) that people aim to stay within their set weight range, but since it is hard to prevent people from striving for thinness in our fat shaming culture, I conceded that they might aim for the lower end *within that range.* For most people, this weight is still heavier than what they consider to be their ideal weight, but I urged people to try to find a way to be okay with it. We've got to get rid of weight stigma and body image concerns, and I do research aiming to move us in that direction, but in the meantime, I suggest that by eating relatively sensibly, and by engaging in recommended amounts of physical activity, people could maintain the weight at the low end of their set range. I called *that* weight the leanest livable weight, by which I meant you would not have to sacrifice your quality of life to maintain it. What I most definitely did not mean is a weight at which you would die if you lost another pound.

I have received a considerable amount of criticism for daring to suggest that obese people could be healthy at their current weight and didn't necessarily have to diet. So I was shocked that morning to read that Goop's readers accused me of the opposite—of telling people to strive to be as thin as life could support. Their complaints spread to wellness blogs, Twitter streams, and ultimately to a legitimate scholar at a prestigious university who continually fanned the flames in public lectures, academic conferences, and comments in several far-reaching newspapers. My own three words were being used to attack me as irresponsible, accusing me of giving dangerous ideas to young girls who were susceptible to eating disorders.

As scientists, we have to be able to defend our conclusions. It's part of the job, starting with oral exams in our graduate training, in which we endure tough questioning from faculty. Responding to lengthy critiques of our manuscripts is a normal and time-consuming stage in the publication process. But defending our conclusions in the public arena is a different beast, and while some people may relish it, I have always dreaded it. For the most part, I've avoided it. I figured my words on the page were my best defense. Until my own words became the problem.

It was agonizing to be accused of being part of the problem I've worked so long to fix, and knowing it was at least partly my own fault made it even worse. To hide away in my comfort zone and not speak up would leave the wrong views out there, uncontested. So I did fight back—by correcting those willfully misconstruing my words, but more importantly by changing what I said. Instead of those three problematic words (which will always and forever be in my book, on pages ix, 31, 90, 169, and twice on 188), I explain that consistently engaging in healthy behavior will make you healthier, even if it doesn't make you thinner, and that health should be the main goal.

As stressful as it is to get the communication right, what's the point of working to discover something new if I am just going to keep it to myself? And as humiliating as this whole experience was, it was helpful to see and correct the disconnection between what I was trying to say about dieting and what others were hearing. If that means more people can use the science to improve their lives rather than to harm themselves, then I might thank the Goop readers for a moment of insight and clarity, rather than cursing them for causing me embarrassment. ■

Traci Mann is professor of psychology at the University of Minnesota, where she founded the Health and Eating Lab. Prior to this, she was a professor at UCLA for 10 years. She is interested in basic science questions about cognitive mechanisms of self-control, in applying social psychology research to promoting healthy behavior, and in busting commonly accepted myths about eating. She is the author of *Secrets from the Eating Lab*, which was the 2016 winner of the Society for Personality and Social Psychology Book Prize.

supporting partner

CONVERGENT
BEHAVIORAL
SCIENCE
INITIATIVE

Congratulations, *Behavioral Scientist*, on bringing even more of your must-read articles into print. From your friends merging design and behavioral science at the University of Virginia.

Visit **convergentbsi.org** to learn more and get in touch.

To Nudge, or Not to Nudge

To nudge, or not to nudge, that isn't the question:
Neither 'tis possible in one's life to avoid
The choice architecture of happenstance,
Nor the plans begot by policy officials,
And opposing, but an illusion. To design—to nudge,
For good; and by a nudge to say we end
The heart-ache and the thousand natural biases
That flesh is heir to: 'tis a consummation
Devoutly to be wish'd. To design, to nudge;
To nudge, perchance to change—ay, there's the rub:
For in that nudge for good what effects may come,
When we have shuffled our mortal subjects,
Must give us pause—there's the respect
Toward agency in so long life.
But who would bear the whips and scorns of time,
Th'oppressor's wrong, the greedy man's ruse,
The pangs of unrealiz'd plans, the law's delay,
The inefficiency of office, and the gaps
That action and intention make,
When we ourselves might our goals attain
With a bare wisdom? Who would burdens bear,
To grunt and sweat toward a weary death,
When that the hope of something more in life,
The undiscovered country, a place which
No society has been, resolves the will,
And makes us rather face those ills we have
Than accept them as permanent?
Thus circumstance doth make nudgers (and nudgees) of us all,
And thus the native hue of irresolution
Is amended with the fresh cast of thought,
And enterprises of great pith and moment
With this regard their currents drive ahead
In the name of actualization.

CHAPTER 7

Re-
Visions

"We shall not cease from exploration
And the end of all our exploring
Will be to arrive where we started
And know the place for the first time."

—T.S. ELIOT

"I start every day with it, in front of the mirror. I say,
Andoumboulouousness. Never failed me yet. It's the
idea that we're hopefully evolving, that we're hopefully
getting better, that we're a draft closer to what we mean
when we say humanity in an idealistic sense."

—NATHANIEL MACKEY

Social Science, Ideology, Culture, & History

By Barry Schwartz

We are, in sum, incomplete or unfinished animals who complete or finish ourselves through culture— and not through culture in general but through highly particular forms of it.

—Clifford Geertz

In 1973, almost a half century ago, distinguished psychologist Kenneth Gergen published an extremely significant and highly controversial article in the prestigious *Journal of Personality and Social Psychology*. The paper was called "Social Psychology as History," and in it, Gergen suggested that the aim of modeling psychological science after the natural sciences was deeply mistaken. It was mistaken because the goal of developing timeless generalizations about your subject was the wrong goal when your subject was human nature. Human beings lived in history and in culture. As history moved and culture changed, human nature changed with it. Whereas it is true that all the phenomena that occupy scientists occur in historical contexts (what are the big bang and the theory of evolution if not theories of natural history, after all), the historical timescale of natural historical events is vast; in contrast, the human timescale is miniscule. One of the questions Gergen raised was whether it made sense to aspire to the kinds of generalizations that physicists sought, or to use the methodological tools that chemists or molecular biologists used, to seek truths about the essentially cultural and historical phenomena that made up human nature. This idea was challenging to his colleagues, to say the least.

But Gergen added another piece to his argument that was even more challenging. If people were essentially historical and cultural creatures, psychologists had to consider one potentially significant part of that culture and history—what people like us, psychological scientists, said about them. We do our research, we develop our theories, we share those theories with colleagues by publishing them, and then what? Do they sit inertly in journals on dusty library shelves, or do they become a part of our culture and history, potentially causing people to behave differently than they did before the theories entered the world. In other words, Gergen was wondering whether our claims about human nature might actually change human nature.

Suppose, for example, that Stanley Milgram's startling studies of the willingness of human beings to obey authority became widely known, as indeed they did. Would that change the way people responded to demands made on them by those in authority? This certainly seems like a plausible possibility. Some people, having been alerted to their tendency to do what they were told, might stiffen their backs and resist. Others might just resign themselves to going along to get along. It could go either way, but whichever way it went, Gergen suggested, the very fact that the Milgram study existed would change the phenomenon that Milgram was trying to understand. And Gergen voiced this concern 50 years ago, when psychologists were not writing national bestsellers and psychological findings leaked from the laboratory into the real world only rarely.

Finding things out in physics is hard. Finding things out in genetics and virology is hard. But at least physicists don't have to worry that their theories of planetary motion will affect how planets move. And at least geneticists and virologists don't have to worry that their theories about genetics and viruses will change how genes and viruses behave in the world. Their theories about planets, genes, and viruses are causally inert. If Gergen is right, this is not true about the theories of psychologists and other behavioral scientists. If Gergen is right, what should psychology (and the other social sciences) look like?

Science, in general, tries to answer "why" questions. It is a systematic attempt to understand and explain. Usually, to understand a domain is to be able to provide some sort of causal explanation of the phenomena in that domain. And often, a test of that causal explanation is science's ability to predict whether similar phenomena will occur in the future, and if so, under what circumstances.

So, scientists might ask, Why do the planets move in their precise orbits around the sun? Why do boats float? Why is the earth getting warmer? Why are viruses killing people? Why do vaccines protect against viruses? Why are prices rising? Why isn't unemployment falling? Why do young kids learn their second languages without an accent? Why do losses have a bigger impact on well-being than do comparably sized gains? Why do police react to nonwhite citizens with hostility and aggression? Why do people misremember what they have experienced? Why do people believe "facts" about the world that are patently untrue?

Science is not unique in its efforts to understand and explain. Many traditional worldviews *also* seek to understand, to explain, and to predict. But science is different. What makes it different? Many years ago, anthropologist Robin Horton sought to answer this question in a careful comparison of scientific thinking and traditional African thinking. He concluded that traditional worldviews were complex, comprehensive, sensitive to evidence, and aimed at finding causes in much the same way that science was. But unlike science, traditional worldviews, influential though they were, had not made much "progress" over the centuries, whereas science had transformed everything it touched. Why? Horton suggested that the "secret sauce" that science alone possessed was a tool of inquiry one did not find in other modes of thought. And that tool was the experiment.

The experiment, typically in the laboratory, allowed you to take a phenomenon from nature and transform the conditions under which it occurred. It allowed you to strip away real life, detail by detail, and observe whether the phenomenon continued to occur unchanged. And if it was changed, changed in what ways? Does fire need oxygen? Imagine a world without oxygen. Would there still be fire? Better yet, create a world without oxygen (in the laboratory) and watch the fire go out. To do an experiment is to imagine a world that is different from the actual world and then build that world and examine what the phenomenon does in that new world. It is to be able to think about the world as it *isn't*—to conjure counterfactuals and then bring them into existence. How creative that is! Imagining counterfactuals is hard enough, but imagining the *right* counterfactuals is harder still. After all, there are infinitely many ways to imagine the world as different from the actual one. Many of these imagined worlds would be silly to contemplate. But some will enable you to find just the causal structure you are looking for.

If experimentation is creative, then experiments are creations. Experiments *invent* facts, or stylize facts, rather than *discovering* them. What I mean is that having found that something is true in the world that you created, you need to show that it is *also* true in the actual world in which you live.

It took me quite some time to come to this view. I was trained in the psychology of B. F. Skinner, perhaps the major figure in mid-twentieth century psychology. Skinner was deeply committed to the view that we could understand almost everything about human behavior by understanding how behavior was affected by rewards and punishments and then analyzing the environment to see which rewards and punishments were operating (see his *Science and Human Behavior*). To develop this view, Skinner invented—created—tightly controlled environments in which simple repetitive behaviors of deprived animals (typically rats or pigeons) could produce outcomes they needed (typically food or water). In these simple environments, manipulation of contingencies between behavior and outcome allowed an extraordinary degree of prediction and control of the animal's behavior. From results obtained in settings like these, Skinner argued that he had created a perfect microcosm for understanding human behavior in the real, complex world. We could understand factory workers pressing slacks for a wage in a clothing factory by studying rats pressing levers for food in a Skinner box. This Skinnerian logic seemed compelling to me. It presented a picture of human nature that I did not find appealing, but there was no arguing with the data.

Or was there? Thanks to the patient and painstaking efforts of Richard Schuldenfrei and Hugh Lacey, two philosopher colleagues of mine at Swarthmore College, I slowly came to believe that the reason Skinner drew the conclusion that rewards and punishments were all that mattered was that he had created a world in which rewards and punishments were all that *could* matter. What was true inside the Skinner box might not be remotely true outside it—unless you engineered the actual world so that it became an extension of the Skinner box. What Schuldenfrei and Lacey taught me is that that is exactly what the industrial revolution, ushered in by market capitalism, had done. Consider what Adam Smith, the founding father of the economic system most of us call home, had to say in 1776:

> It is in the inherent interest of every man to live as much at his ease as he can; and if his emoluments are to be precisely the same whether he does or does not perform some very laborious duty, to perform it in as careless and slovenly a manner that authority will permit.

In other words, people work for pay—nothing more and nothing less. Smith's belief in the power of rewards led him to argue for organizing work by dividing labor into simple, easily

If Gergen is right, then at least in the social sciences, theories, rather than being beholden to facts, can shape facts in a way that strengthens the theories.

repeated, essentially meaningless units, much like the lever presses of rats or the key pecks of pigeons. As long as people were getting paid for what they did, it didn't matter very much what their jobs entailed. And by dividing labor into little bits, society would gain enormous productive efficiency. In extolling the virtues of the division of labor, Smith offered a description of a pin factory that has become famous:

> One man draws out the wire, another straits it, a third cuts it, a fourth points it, a fifth grinds it at the top for receiving the head ... I have seen a small manufactory of this kind where ten men only were employed ... They could make among them upwards of forty-eight thousand pins a day ... But if they had all wrought separately and independently ... they certainly could not, each of them, make twenty.

You might ask why anyone would choose to work in Smith's pin factory, putting heads on pins, minute after minute, hour after hour, day after day. Smith's answer was that of course, people wouldn't enjoy working in the pin factory. But they wouldn't enjoy working anywhere. What Smith was telling us is that the only reason people do any kind of work is for the payoffs it produces. And as long as it produces adequate payoffs, what the work itself consists of doesn't matter.

More than a century later, the same view guided Frederick Winslow Taylor, the father of what came to be called the "scientific management" movement. Taylor used meticulous time and motion studies to refine the factory, as envisioned by Smith, so that human laborers were essentially part of a well-oiled machine. And he designed compensation schemes that pushed employees to work hard, work fast, and work accurately.

Then, a generation later, along came Skinner. And Skinner created in the laboratory a world that was modeled on the world that had been created in the factory. But the factory was an invention—a creation—just as was the Skinner box. The question that was left unanswered, or with the answer presumed, was how much this invented world captured human nature in the actual world. It was at least possible that the created world had rather little to tell us about the actual world, *except perhaps that the actual world could be transformed into a version of the created world.*

And this brings us back to Gergen's argument about people as cultural and historical creatures. When done right, science is an ongoing conversation between theory and data. The point of theories in science is to organize and explain the facts. Facts without organizing theories are close to useless. But theories must ultimately be accountable to the facts. And new facts force us to modify or discard inadequate theories.

That's the ideal. But if Gergen is right, then at least in the social sciences, theories, rather than being beholden to facts, can shape facts in a way that strengthens the theories.

"If you build it, they will come." This is the mantra that the main character in the movie *Field of Dreams* keeps hearing as he turns his farmland into a baseball park in the middle of nowhere. He builds it, and they *do* come. I want to suggest, influenced by Gergen, that at least sometimes, when social scientists build theories, the people come. That is, the people may be nudged into behaving in ways that support the theories.

In other contexts, this is familiar territory. Does the market cater to consumer desires or does it create consumer desires? Do the media cater to people's tastes in news and entertainment or do the media create those tastes? Whenever we encounter markets creating demand, or media creating tastes, we are encountering a version of the process articulated by Gergen.

Ideas about human nature that are false when they are made can *become* true as social institutions, like workplaces, become shaped by them.

Adam Smith's ideas about human laziness helped give shape to the industrial revolution. As economic historian Karl Polanyi pointed out in *The Great Transformation*, people's conceptions of economic activity prior to the industrial revolution were very different than they were after the revolution, as was the form and manner of the work they did. Smith might have been wrong about people when he wrote *The Wealth of Nations*. But the monumentally influential book ushered in a set of changes in the economic and cultural landscape that made his ideas true. Said another way, Smith's idea about human nature—his "invention" or "creation"—was a piece of technology every bit as world changing as a microchip, a search engine, or a social network.

But there is something special about this technology of ideas. Search engines and microchips don't change the world unless they work. Ideas, in contrast, can have a major impact on human life even when they are false. Adam Smith's conception of human beings as lazy was untrue. People want to work and they want to work well. They put effort into what they do, and take pride in excellent results (I make a an extended argument along these lines in my book *Why We Work*). Yet if the only work available to people is in places like Smith's pin factory (or a modern call center or fulfillment center), then his account of human nature starts to look true—starts to *be* true. Why else would one work in a pin factory except for the wage? Why would one work carefully and diligently unless one's wage depended on it? And why would a rat press a lever, or a person press a pair of slacks, except for the payoff it produced? Skinner created a laboratory setting in which nothing but payoffs could matter. His was a psychology of the assembly line. And if all we see around us is one or another version of the assembly line, then our behavior will come to resemble the behavior of Skinner's rats.

Karl Marx used the term "false consciousness" or "ideology" to label such incorrect ideas. The term "ideology" has not been used consistently over time. The term's history began in France in the eighteenth century, coined to denote a "science of ideas." People whom the French emperor Napoleon termed *ideologues* were so in love with ideas that they ignored empirical evidence, sometimes right in front of their noses, that might contradict those ideas. A more recent manifestation of this view of people as so committed to ideas that they ignore evidence can be found in Jonathan Haidt's *The Righteous Mind*, which argues that people's moral commitments stem not from reason and reflection but from deep-seated intuitions of which they are largely unaware. That is, people use reason to make a case for what they already believe, as a lawyer does—not to tell them what they ought to believe, as a judge does. This orientation can lead not only to ignoring evidence but to distorting it, a result of what psychologist Lee Ross called "naïve realism." The naïve realist is someone who thinks that "I see things as they are; people who disagree with me are distorting the truth." For Marx, ideologues weren't just ignoring evidence to preserve their pet theories; they were *distorting* evidence to conform to what they already believed, or were conditioned by their circumstances to believe, or wanted to believe. And beyond distorting evidence, in line with the Gergen's suggestion that ideas, in the form of scientific theories, can change reality, ideas about human nature that are false when they are made can *become* true as social institutions, like workplaces, become shaped by them.

Adam Smith seemed to know this. He writes, in *The Wealth of Nations*:

> The man whose life is spent in a few simple operations . . . has no occasion to exert his understanding, or to exercise his invention in finding out expedients for difficulties which never occur. He naturally loses, therefore, the habit of such exertion and generally becomes as stupid and ignorant as it is possible for a human creature to be.

The key things to notice about this statement are the words "loses" and "becomes." Here is Smith, the father of the assumption that people are basically lazy and work only for pay, saying that work in a factory will cause people to "lose" something, and "become" something. So what is it that they *had* before entering the factory that they "lost"? And what is it that they *were* before entering the factory that was different from what they "became"? Right here in this quote we see evidence that Smith believed that what people were like as workers depended on the conditions of their work. And yet, over the years, this nuanced understanding of human nature as the product of the human environment got lost, or forgotten.

So, ideas change people. The pressing question is how. How can a technology of ideas take root, even when the ideas are false—even when they are ideology?

I think there are three basic dynamics through which false ideas can become true. The first way ideology becomes true is by *reconstrual*—by changing how people think about and understand their own actions. For example, someone who volunteered every week in a homeless shelter might one day read a book that tells him it is human nature to be selfish. He might then say to himself, "I thought I was acting altruistically. Now social scientists are telling me that I work in a homeless shelter for ego gratification."

The second mechanism by which ideology becomes true is via what is called the *self-fulfilling prophecy*. Here, ideology changes how other people respond to the actor, which, in turn, changes what the actor does in the future. The phrase "self-fulfilling prophecy" was coined by sociologist Robert Merton in 1948. He discussed examples of how theories that initially do not describe the world accurately can become descriptive if they are acted upon. In essence, a self-fulfilling prophecy is, in the beginning, "a *false* definition of the situation evoking a new behavior that makes the originally false conception come *true.*"

These two mechanisms might be expected to have only minor effects; they are changing people's conceptions of themselves "retail," i.e., one person at a time. Can ideology also work "wholesale," at scale? This brings me to the final mechanism by which ideology can have an influence. When institutional structures are changed in a way that is consistent with the ideology, they can change everyone and everything. The industrialist believes that workers are only motivated to work by wages and then constructs an assembly line that reduces work to such meaningless bits that there is no reason to work aside from the wages. When social structures are shaped by ideology, ideology can change the world.

I have argued here that the social sciences are delivering to us something less than they hope. Rather than giving us timeless truths, they give us evidence of what may be true in a particular time and place, but not in all times and places. Indeed, one of the factors that may affect the generality of what the social sciences tell us is the very fact that they are telling us. (That indeed was Gergen's point.)

One response to my argument is, "Duh! Who doesn't know this?" Fair enough. Everyone working in the social sciences knows that what they find has boundary conditions. This limitation is so obvious that it doesn't need to be stated. Even Newtonian mechanics has boundary conditions. But in the case of human nature and human behavior (unlike the motions of planets and falling apples), those boundary conditions may be so important and so dynamic that simply leaving them unstated and largely unexplored is leaving most of what needs to be understood invisible.

The social sciences need to be sciences where boundary conditions are at the center of the action. This is one of the things that anthropologist Clifford Geertz had in mind when he called human beings "unfinished animals." Culture changes us, and as culture changes, our natures change as well. So the attempt to get to the bottom of human nature must include an attempt to understand the way in which people are embedded in culture and history.

You might think that living, as we are, in what some have called a "post-truth" culture, in which everything (e.g., global warming, vaccine efficacy, electoral results, the size of crowds at presidential inaugurations) is up for grabs, the last thing we need is another assault on the credibility of science. So let me be clear. Even if we are living in a post-truth world, I am not suggesting that we should be. I am not suggesting that truth is socially constructed—that you have your truths and I have mine. What I *am* suggesting is that human nature is socially constructed. This is what it means to say, as Geertz does, that "culture finishes us." The tools of science are certainly fallible (some suggest that the history of science is just one damn mistake after another), but science can find out, like no other activity in human history, what the truth is at a particular moment in a particular place. We should respect

Rather than giving us timeless truths, the social sciences give us evidence of what may be true in a particular time and place, but not in all times and places. Indeed, one of the factors that may affect the generality of what the social sciences tell us is the very fact that they are telling us.

empirical evidence while at the same time asking ourselves about the limits of its applicability. And we should be ruthless in our criticism of those who blithely ignore empirical evidence, or flat-out contradict it.

We can also build into our methods an explicit appreciation of culture and history. The discipline of cultural psychology already does this, welcoming the serious study of culture into the psychological universe. The same can be done for history. Empirical evidence from history should inform the kinds of theories psychologists construct. Is there controversy and uncertainty among historians? Of course there is. But there is controversy and uncertainty among those who get their truths from the laboratory. Fallibility, not certainty. Fallibility, not nihilism.

Nobel Prize–winning economist Robert Shiller recently suggested, in his book *Narrative Economics*, that the best way to understand people and the institutions with which they live is historical. People make sense of the world by telling themselves stories—stories about where they were, where they are, and where they are going. These stories tend to be headed somewhere, not falling back on themselves. There are always new inputs that change the shape of existing institutions and thus change the direction of people's stories. Society is what might be called an "open" system, in which phenomena created by social structures and practices at one point in time become causal agents that shape new practices going forward. In the present moment, for example, the explosion of social media has introduced influences on us that no previous efforts to understand human nature had to cope with. My bet is that the human world will never again be what it was even twenty years ago.

Our narrative—our history—helps us make sense of the present, even if it does not allow us to predict the future. (As some critics of economics like to point out, economists have predicted nine of the last three recessions!) Our narrative helps us to understand. Science has a prominent role to play in shaping that narrative and informing that understanding, but only if we properly understand what science can do—and what it can't. Science at its best helps us develop the most perspicuous narratives, the most compelling understanding. But it does not offer proof. Experiments are not "facts" that must be incorporated into any account so much as demonstrations—creations—that may guide our forming narratives in ways that mere observation can't match. But they will only play this role when they are aided by the creative and imaginative interpretations of researchers who are trying to develop the best narrative they can of the current state of human nature and human society. ∎

Barry Schwartz is a visiting professor at Haas School of Business, U.C. Berkeley, emeritus professor of psychology at Swarthmore College, and the author of *The Paradox of Choice*, *Why We Work*, and *Practical Wisdom* (with Kenneth Sharpe).

Disclosure: Barry Schwartz is a member of the Behavioral Scientist's *advisory board.*

PART 7

Journey to Robbers Cave

SIMILAR TO OTHER well-known social psychology studies of the mid—twentieth century—such as Stanley Milgram's "shock box" obedience experiments—Sherif conceived the camp studies as a direct response to the Second World War and other global conflicts. Social psychologists of the postwar era struggled to make sense of the horrors of the Holocaust by researching human conformity, obedience to authority, and intergroup relations.

Today, the camp studies are remembered as classic examples of the field study method, as well as for their overarching examination of intergroup relations. Echoing how the results were published, people generally focus on the 1954 camp at Robbers Cave State Park, and mention the 1949 and 1953 camps in passing, if at all. Those reporting on the studies typically assign Muzafer Sherif (and occasionally Carolyn Wood Sherif) sole credit, overlooking his many collaborators across the three camps.

But in more recent years, serious questions have been raised about the ethics of these postwar researchers, particularly their collective decision to conceal from participants the true purpose of their research. Contemporary reviews of the camp studies regularly invoke William Golding's book Lord of the Flies (coincidentally published the same year as the Robbers Cave camp), although unlike in the book, the conflict between groups was artificially and purposefully created by Sherif and his team, rather than having emerged naturally. Central to the criticism are questions of the transparency of the original research reports. Gina Perry's 2018 book The Lost Boys has perhaps ignited the heaviest round of concern as she revealed in a series of interviews with former campers that not only were they unaware that their camp days had been part of psychological research but also that several of the boys attributed some enduring discomfort to the memories of the experience. Deceiving the boys about the true nature of their camp had never been secret; Sherif and his colleagues believed it was essential that the boys be unaware that

Purpose of the Camp

For many years camp executives throughout the country have been trying to find out what camp activities will result in giving their campers a fruitful educational and recreational experience. These camp directors are interested in finding out what things can be done to give their boys and girls a wholesome cooperative living experience which will prepare the youngsters for better citizenship and to be leaders in their communities. The question is what camp programs best serve to enrich the life and experience of growing children?

In view of this the purpose of the camp is simply to study the best programs and procedures for campers which will develop cooperative and spiritual living. A grant has been obtained ~~_____~~ to study the programs and camp activities of a regularly operated and established camp. This year we are operating Camp Talualac and it is being directed by Dr. Marvin B. Sussman of Union College with the advice and counsel of various Camp Directors, and other experts from the University of Oklahoma and Yale.

Description of the purpose of the camp studies provided to parents in 1953.

Handwritten publication edits prepared by Muzafer Sherif in 1966. "What is needed is a world organization whose principles are held binding ... a world organization which can apply sanctions even to the mightiest & wealthiest nations [and likes of nations] when they take the law into their own hands in an ethnocentric way. But there are certain prerequisites for such viable and effective world organization."

the camp was anything but a regular summer camp. This point was emphasized in planning documents, instructions to observers and camp counselors, and in communications with parents. But the boys were never debriefed, instead learning of the deception when Perry approached them for interviews, just over half a century later.

For their part, parents knew from the beginning that they were sending their children to an atypical summer camp. Consent forms, informational letters, and in-person information sessions explained that the camp was being run for the purposes of research. The true purpose of that research and what the study would entail were less clear. Researchers told parents that the camp would provide a "wholesome cooperative living experience" that would "prepare the youngsters for better citizenship and to be leaders in their communities." There was never mention of purposefully engineering conflict with other campers, nor the overarching search for a solution to global conflict.

Perhaps more striking among concerns of the transparency surrounding the camp studies is that a careful reading of Sherif's original footnotes by Frances Cherry in 1995 re-exposed why the second camp in 1953 had been called off. In his own writing, Sherif initially acknowledged that the study had been cut short after the boys discovered the experimental ruse. In later accounts, Sherif changed how he framed the 1953 study, citing "unfavorable conditions" and "errors in judgment" on the part of the researchers for its early conclusion, and obscuring that the cleverness of his young subjects was the real reason why the two groups of campers never completed the conflict stage.

Critics have also raised additional questions concerning the way the researchers merged results of the three studies. Psychology students have often been introduced to the studies through confident statements about the dynamics of group formation, intergroup conflict, and how working toward a common goal can bring peaceful resolution—but these are the results only of the 1954 Robbers Cave camp. In 1949, the groups failed to resolve their conflict; in 1953, the study was cut short. Much like in the real world, conflict in an experiment proved to be complex, an important nuance that receives little attention amid the work's greater legacy.

In spite of the criticisms, it cannot be said that Sherif shied away from trying to put his work to use for a greater good. With the outbreak of the Korean and Vietnam wars on the heels of the Second World War and the growing threat of the Cold War, the Sherifs' work

A drawing from a boy at the 1953 camp featuring two teams engaged in a tug-of-war, complete with a figure armed with a starter pistol.

was a direct attempt to resolve the problems consuming the world. Carolyn herself reflected that it should be no surprise that a Turkish psychologist who witnessed the atrocities of war firsthand as the Ottoman Empire fell in his youth only to find himself exiled from his homeland after marrying an American should come to study global conflict.

In his notes and publications, Muzafer was cautious to never lay blame on individuals for global hostilities, instead focusing on groups—nations, governments—that he spent his career seeking to understand through the observation of group dynamics among children and adolescents. To pave the path to harmony, he called for a world organization with the power to hold even the strongest nations accountable. Today, the question remains as to whether a new generation of social scientists will take up the optimism and ambition of the Sherifs' vision and bring new solutions to the world stage. ∎

Select References

· Muzafer and Carolyn Wood Sherif papers. Drs. Nicholas and Dorothy Cummings Center for the History of Psychology, The University of Akron, Akron, OH.

· Sherif, M., Harvey, O. J., White, B. J., Hood, W. R., & Sherif, C. W. (1961). *Intergroup conflict and cooperation: The Robbers Cave experiment.* Norman, OK: University of Oklahoma Book Exchange.

· Perry, G. (2018). *The lost boys: Inside Muzafer Sherif's Robbers Cave experiment.* Victoria, Australia: Scribe.

· Cherry, F. E. (1995). *The 'stubborn particulars' of social psychology: Essays on the research process.* New York, NY: Routledge.

Dulce et Decorum Est
By Wilfred Owen

Bent double, like old beggars under sacks,
Knock-kneed, coughing like hags, we cursed through sludge,
Till on the haunting flares we turned our backs,
And towards our distant rest began to trudge.
Men marched asleep. Many had lost their boots,
But limped on, blood-shod. All went lame; all blind;
Drunk with fatigue; deaf even to the hoots
Of gas-shells dropping softly behind.

Gas! GAS! Quick, boys!—An ecstasy of fumbling
Fitting the clumsy helmets just in time,
But someone still was yelling out and stumbling
And flound'ring like a man in fire or lime.—
Dim through the misty panes and thick green light,
As under a green sea, I saw him drowning.

In all my dreams before my helpless sight,
He plunges at me, guttering, choking, drowning.

If in some smothering dreams, you too could pace
Behind the wagon that we flung him in,
And watch the white eyes writhing in his face,
His hanging face, like a devil's sick of sin;
If you could hear, at every jolt, the blood
Come gargling from the froth-corrupted lungs,
Obscene as cancer, bitter as the cud
Of vile, incurable sores on innocent tongues,—
My friend, you would not tell with such high zest
To children ardent for some desperate glory,
The old Lie: *Dulce et decorum est*
Pro patria mori.

Dulce et decorum est pro patria mori: It is sweet and fitting to die for one's country.

Is Everything BS?

By Rory Sutherland

Is everything BS?

Taking BS to mean behavioral science, the answer to that question is, not quite. But most things are. Most things involve a heavy dose of behavioral science. I would argue, however, the contrary does not apply. I don't want us to start thinking that BS is everything. It is necessary but not sufficient in many, many cases.

I'd add that BS (behavioral science) without creativity—indeed BS without a tiny little whiff of BS (meaning bullshit)—may be actually suboptimal. If you don't use behavioral science to expand the potential solution space to a problem by adding a psychological dimension in addition to the other aspects or metrics you're considering, you're probably missing a huge opportunity.

This is the vital thing: to a great extent, I think everything is BS. There are huge numbers of problems that persist in the world and that probably could be solved much more quickly if people would consider a behavioral or psychological dimension. At the same time, I don't want us to make the opposite mistake—to immediately go in, look at a problem, and assume that it has to be solved exclusively by the application of behavioral science. A lot of things are a mixture.

If you look at medicine, one of the slightly strange things about it is that they subtract the placebo effect. Now, given that the placebo effect can contribute to a cure, or to the efficacy of a treatment, you'd think people would be trying to actually maximize the placebo effect. What medicine does is say, "We subtract the psychological component of the efficacy of a treatment from the overall efficacy and what remains is the science." Now, that seems a dubious thing to do. It seems to be self-evident that there are lots of cases where a beneficial combination of a psychological placebo effect and medicinal treatment would be the best solution of all.

One of the great quotes I always use—which, when I first saw it on a PowerPoint slide, I thought was a bit banal, but I now realize is incredibly important—is Harry Truman's quote, "It is amazing what you can accomplish if you do not care who gets the credit." Quite a lot of science is so desperate to prove the efficacy of what it itself does—the drugs company can't claim credit for the placebo effect, they can only claim credit for the medicinal component of the treatment—that we become fixated on proving what we can do alone at the expense of proving and optimizing what we can do together.

Let's take something really simple: a sale in a shop. Now, if you're a mainstream economist you would look at a sale and you would say, "Well, this is perfectly clear and consistent with mainstream economic theory; you reduce the prices of things and demand goes up." To some degree, that's true. I think if you held a sale and you didn't drop the prices, you could do all the other stuff, and I think people would be fairly pissed off.

But equally, I don't think it's fair to say that a sale only works through effectively tweaking the price-demand curve. There are lots of things going on with a sale—there's scarcity value, the fear that other people might buy the shit that you want, social proof in that there are huge queues of people outside the shop waiting to get in, and an additional element of scarcity in that most sales, although there are exceptions to this, last for a finite length of time. There is a shop on Oxford Street that's been holding a closing down sale uninterruptedly for about the last five years, but that caters to tourists who aren't around to notice the inconsistency.

So the most important thing you can do with a sale is not purely the economic bit, and it's not purely the behavioral bit. It's both. And in medicine, the best thing you can do is probably combine the drug's psychological and pharmacological sides.

We need to start making friends with lots of other people who understand that solving problems is more complex and leaves more scope for creativity than the standard models currently allow.

Let me show you what I mean by this.

If I gave you and a team of people two candles and I said, "You have to boil this quantity of water using only the candles and a box of matches," people would probably struggle. And then some shrewd people will come in and say, "Well, actually, this is impossible, because look, the calorific value of the candles is insufficient to heat this volume of water to a point where it actually boils."

So, you put a big tick in the box saying "cannot be done." And you move on to the next question.

Of course, it's not quite true, is it? Because the boiling point of water depends on altitude, you could take it to a very, very high place and the same calorific value might well boil the water. If you actually produced a vacuum around the water, it'd be easier still. Or, as another compromise, you could just move the water to France, where, as everybody knows, water boils at 50 degrees. That's the only thing that explains the shit quality of the tea, to be honest.

There are lots of ways you can solve the problem by simply recontextualizing it and adding new variables to the mix. We rarely notice these things. A lot of people will say, "Okay, this is impossible," because they've failed to add what you might call the altitude or the air pressure component to the mix of variables needing to be considered.

I think there are whole categories in business like this, where some of the world's greatest geniuses have solved extraordinary engineering problems but have completely failed to take the psychological component into account.

Think of solar panels. I don't think anybody can fail to be extraordinarily impressed by the improvements made with solar panels in terms of their efficiency, the lower cost to manufacture them, the lower weight. And improvements continue to be made, beyond the point people thought was feasible a few years ago. Engineers have solved that problem, and, geniuses as they are, they deserve credit for doing that. But businesses have missed what you might call air pressure in the equation. They've missed, "How the hell do we sell this to people so they put it on the goddamn roof." It is assumed, still, that solar panels are sold in one irreversible decision to somebody who fixes it irremovably onto their roof with a one percent chance that everything could go totally shit; either your local electricity provider refuses to pay for the electricity you put in or your roof starts collapsing under the weight or you discover you've got some hideous problem with beetles.

Now, what we know about humans is they hate making irreversible, five-figure decisions. They really, really hate making those kinds of decisions. So you've solved all of the scientific problems, you've got the whole how-to-maximize-the-calorific-value-out-of-the-candle stuff done, but you've failed to spot the fact that there's another problem out there that you still have to solve before you can actually have a meaningful effect on personal energy consumption and on mass energy generation.

Nuclear power, you could argue, is even more extreme in that they completely screwed the pooch by choosing the word nuclear, which was associated with bombs, to describe the form of power generation, which it has very little in common with.

If you change the psychological frame in which people have to decide, if you change the context, if you change the story, it's exactly the same as changing air pressure—you change what happens.

The other point I make is when you're dealing with the rules of physics, they're written somewhere upstairs. You can't change them. Data from the past is necessary and sufficient to explaining what the laws might be in the future, because the laws of physics don't change (at least at the scale we experience the world). In contrast, the laws of human behavior are highly context dependent, and they change according to things as strange as fashion, whim, storytelling, and mood.

Obsessing about the extent to which something you try in the future must make sense in terms of data you have from the past is a massive constraint on innovation and experimentation. In physics, yes, if it didn't work in the past, it probably won't work in the future, and the laws tell you what is impossible.

In anything involving psychology, and, you might argue, certain things involving complex systems, actually trying the same thing again and again and again with the expectation that it might work one time is not necessarily a definition of insanity; it might be a definition of complexity.

Once you accept the fact that we can't necessarily focus all our time on how to steer the ship in situations where we can also change the weather, or in which the weather can change in ways we don't expect, we move away from this kind of deterministic, rationalistic obsession with things that make sense in advance.

That's one of my final creative lessons for behavioral science. Don't just test the things that make sense. Test the things that don't make any sense. Then, if you find that they work, you've learned something valuable. Actually, you've learned something mega valuable, because it's something that nobody else knows, because the odds are nobody else has been wacko enough to test it.

We did a charity mailing where we tested seven different variables. The one rational one that made sense to everybody was a goddamn disaster. It actually reduced donations by about 30 to 40 percent. All the ones that were wacko improved the level of donation. This is the really important point about creativity: there are far more good ideas out there we can post-rationalize than there are good ideas we can pre-rationalize. The subset of things that we can try that haven't been tried before that makes sense in advance is very, very small compared to the subset of things that might work in different circumstances.

The bizarre half-sister of creativity is testing and rigorous measurement. They seem like the most different things in the world but they're actually interdependent. Let me explain how things actually make no sense at all in until you try them.

If I suggest to you that you should get two dishwashers, nearly everybody, either who doesn't have two dishwashers or who doesn't have an evangelist friend with two dishwashers, is going to look at me as if I am totally barking insane. But here's the weird thing: if you have two dishwashers, you never need to unload the dishwasher, and you don't actually lose any storage space. Because you have a dirty dishwasher, which is where the dirty stuff goes, and you retrieve stuff from the clean dishwasher, eat off it, put it in the dirty dishwasher. When the dirty dishwasher is full, you turn it on, you put the post-it-note that says "clean" on that dishwasher, and then you simply reverse the process. There's no unloading necessary. There's no storage lost.

What's weird is that this occurs to absolutely nobody in advance. It is absolutely obvious in retrospect, but it's completely nonobvious in advance. And this is why we need creativity and what I call the benign bullshit part of bullshit in behavioral science. Stop obsessing about temperature, the volume of water, and the calorific power of the candles—let's look for some other variables we might want to introduce.

I didn't learn any of this at university, I learned it all at Ogilvy. What university teaches you to do is reduce every problem into a two-body problem, which can be solved mathematically to a single, optimal, right answer. Pretend that the problem is that simple, solve for the pretend simplistic model, and then pat yourself on the back. It was only at Ogilvy that I learned, No, the trick here is to go and find some completely different variable that no one's looking at and try messing around with that instead.

I had a wonderful experience when Daniel Kahneman emailed me and about six or seven other people with exactly the kind of problem we ought to be looking at it. Someone had told Daniel, "A friend of mine sells fruit and vegetables at a farmers market somewhere in Austin,

the very end, I realized that what we were all doing was the same thing that economists would have done. Economists would have said, "It's very simple, you drop the price." If you're an economist, you're looking at a particular set of variables, which are high-status variables. We were all looking at it through the lens of scarcity value.

Maybe it's something completely different. Maybe it's the end of the day and the bloke towards the end of the day is just losing interest a bit and he just doesn't look that interested in his customers and he starts packing things into the van and then the table is now half covered, so it looks like you're not supposed to be buying from him. It's one of the things we have to explore. And it has to be tested as well.

This is the really important point about creativity: there are far more good ideas out there we can post-rationalize than there are good ideas we can pre-rationalize.

Texas, and he makes pretty large margins"— because, I guess, he's selling to hipsters, where the lumpier and more deformed the vegetables are, the more they'll pay—"but the problem is that he can never quite sell out."

As Richard Thaler rightly explained to the group, scarcity value applies with perhaps pallets of strawberries, and it applies with electrical goods, which are all identical. But with single vegetables and fruit, we tend to assume the last cucumber is probably a bit manky and unwanted, and no one wants to buy it.

Here you had a bunch of people all answering this fundamentally fascinating question about how to sell your last bit of fruit. There were various suggestions, all fascinating. At

When I wrote my book, I said that if you run a coffee shop, leave the chairs and tables outside even if it's raining, because from 300 yards away the fact that you have tables and chairs on the pavement signals that you're open, it means there's coffee available, because if you closed you would have put the chairs away.

Someone wrote to me and said they used to use that exact insight in reverse. This person worked for a coffee shop and the last thing they wanted was bastards coming in in the last 15 minutes before closing time and ordering a coffee and then sitting around for 45 minutes. Coffee shop owners all over the world are going to hate me for sharing this—all you've got to do is take two chairs, stack them upside down on a table.

Obsessing about the extent to which something you try in the future must make sense in terms of data you have from the past is a massive constraint on innovation and experimentation.

No one comes in and no one orders a goddamn thing. Simply having two chairs upside down—you haven't said closed, you haven't changed the sign—simply doing that tiny little thing is basically enough to prevent anybody coming into your coffee shop.

What we have to do, effectively, is an element of decision hygiene. We've got a very, very weird decision-making process, where the deterministic and the reductionist comes first and the creativity, if it's admitted at all, comes last.

Look at how government proceeds. It starts off with legislation, then if legislation fails, it moves to economic incentives. If economic incentives fail, it moves on to persuasion. Well, you don't have to be a libertarian to say that's completely the wrong way around.

What we need is a long period of recontextualizing the problem through the lens of complexity, the lens of psychology, the lens of behavioral economics, the lens of economics, and the lens of legislation. Drug times placebo is much better than drug or placebo on its own. How do we multiply these various things to actually solve the problem without artificially narrowing it into terms of your imagined high-status solution and implementing that?

When I first met Daniel, in 2009, he said, "I have no hope that we'll actually make human behavior more rational. What I do hope is that we get more conversation around how people make decisions." See, people will start saying, "Well, I think I'm going to go on holiday, but I'm wondering if it's sunk-cost bias, because I've already paid the deposit." As Daniel said back then, if we can simply change how people gossip, if we can change the way people discuss problems so that opening it up to other fields and other variables is seen as a positive, not as a disruption, then we've made 90 percent of the progress we need.

I've occasionally sat on a board as a nonexecutive director. Do not put a marketing person on a board. Seriously, marketing people will hate me for this; have a separate board for these discussions. There are 10 people all going, "This product isn't selling, so we need to drop the price." I'm sitting at the back and what I want to say is, "Have you thought about making it pink?" I know the second I say this it'll be like passing wind, it'll be a social embarrassment, all my status will disappear.

If we can rebalance the status of different modes of problem solving, and we can operate these things in parallel rather than in series, we'll make progress. Just add a bit of creativity, acknowledge that yes, everything is BS, but BS isn't everything, and actually allow space for the other kind of BS. A little bit of bullshit when you're dealing with a future you can't predict or fully understand is highly permissible. ∎

This essay was adapted from a talk given at Nudgestock 2021.

Rory Sutherland is the vice chairman of Ogilvy in the U.K., an attractively vague job title which has allowed him to cofound a behavioral science practice within the agency. Before founding Ogilvy's behavioral science practice, Rory was a copywriter and creative director at Ogilvy for over 20 years. He is the author of *Alchemy: The Surprising Power of Ideas That Don't Make Sense*.

We are grateful for the support of our 2021 organizational sponsors and donors:

WISE OWLS

INVESTORS

Behavioral Science in a Future, Far, Far Away

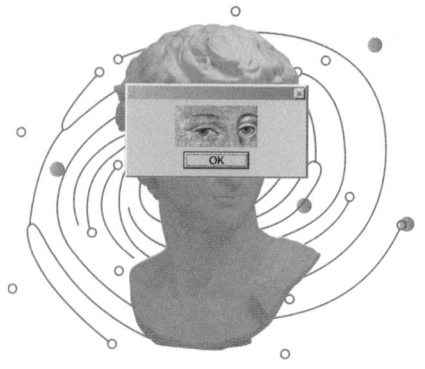

It was only a few hundred thousand years ago that we, *Homo sapiens*, began our journey as a unique species. In that time, we developed sufficient cognitive sophistication to bring about behavioral modernity, which in turn enabled nearly eight billion of us to now inhabit the Earth and transform it to our needs and wants (for better and worse).

One of the pinnacles of our accomplishments is the development of science as a method to apprehend the universe. The seeds of modern scientific thinking germinated with the ancients, but it was not until much later, some three to four hundred years ago, that the modern scientific method began to be applied widely to our understanding of the natural world.

Longer still was the wait for us to turn a scientific gaze upon ourselves.

In wasn't until the late 1800s that the first formal psychological laboratory was formed. Much of the focus in these early days was on investigating the nature of our sensations and perception. Those early experiments helped us understand how our internal experience relates to physical reality—for instance, finding the smallest level of a stimulus we can detect. Soon, the scope of study expanded to include concepts like learning, memory, and our social worlds. Philosopher and psychologist Edna Heidbreder described psychology as "interesting, if for no other reason, because it affords a spectacle of a science still in the making."

Over the next century and a half, this science-in-the-making grew quickly. The field tackled tougher and tougher problems, moving beyond probing the basic mechanisms of behavior to questioning how complex cognitive and emotional systems interact. Major discoveries came along the way, illuminating the bounded nature of our rationality, the profound impacts of social influence on our decision-making, and the connection between our brain activity and our behavior. It all coalesced to propel our knowledge of the human brain, behavior, and mind forward. In turn, this knowledge has accelerated the rate behavioral insights are being deployed in areas central to our lives, like public policy, education, and health.

But the history of our science, like our history as a species, is miniscule relative to what lies ahead. We've turned a scientific eye toward ourselves for only a tiny fraction of one percent of human existence. In the thousands of millennia to come, what might we expect to learn about ourselves, and how might we apply that knowledge?

Accurately predicting the future in the long run seems impossible, not least because we're poor at predicting on shorter timescales. But that doesn't make prospection futile. By envisioning what the distant future might bring, we can begin to uncover the kinds of questions the science of human behavior will be called upon to answer.

Deepening immersion in the digital world

An obvious place to start is how we interact with and immerse ourselves in technology. Today, we extend our minds with devices like smartphones and convene in virtual rather than physical offices. For many, entertainment and social connection comes through online, rather than in-person, activity. As our technology progresses, it seems an eventuality that a central feature of the human experience will be the metaverse,

By

Nathaniel Barr
and
Kelly Peters

a digital, interoperable, and immersive virtual world. A virtual world where we might work, shop, socialize, and even travel.

As the lines between our physical and digital lives fade, fundamental questions about what it means to be human will arise. How might our conception of our identity change if we interact in our physical form less often than as our virtual avatars? How will our definitions of our social relationships, like that of a spouse or friend, be transformed? To what extent will individuals differ in their preference to live, work, and play in the physical or digital realms—might there be segments who reside primarily in one and not the other, leading to groups of humans occupying distinct realities, rarely interacting?

Moving beyond the mental and physical limits that have defined our species

Similar questions will arise as new technology allows us to transcend our physical and mental limits. As humans, much of our existence is governed by these boundaries. We get old. We only grow so tall or run so fast. We can only process so much information. Our ability to learn something new is constrained by our rate of learning and the time it takes to practice. We can't do it all. Indeed, much of our early scientific study of humans involved finding and documenting these limits.

Now imagine that biomedical engineering increases our average lifespan to 200 or genetic or cybernetic interventions massively increase our intelligence; that we can reduce or eliminate the need for sleep; that adjusting our height or personality becomes as easy as selecting the attributes of a video game character. What if one day we achieve an existence entirely free from our biological constraints? Or we psychoengineer away the cognitive biases and myopic tendencies that we focus on so much today?

Certainly, the idea of what it means to be human will shift. If anyone can become a polymath or a bodybuilder, how do we think of concepts like intelligence, talent, or perseverance? If elements of our minds and bodies that once were a function of genetics and life experience become more like a consumer choice, how will we come to view each other, knowing that our identities were selected rather than determined? Will such

a future of choice be segregated to only a select few or made accessible to all?

And if the technologies we apply to ourselves in the future update as frequently as our phones today, what will this continual, rapid update of human ability mean for the shelf life of insights from the behavioral sciences?

Technology that outpaces its ethical application

With new possibilities come new ethical conundrums. In *Jurassic Park*, Ian Malcolm quips that "scientists were so preoccupied with whether or not they could, they didn't stop to think if they should." With rapid technological development opening us to so much potential change, are we already on the path to creating something we wish we hadn't? For precedent, consider the polarizing effects of social media and the perverse incentives of the attention economy. When creating new technology, humans might do well to ask, "Should we?" more often.

Behavioral scientists of the future may similarly struggle with the question of how far behavioral science should go. The ethics of applied behavioral science is already on people's minds, whether in the context of nudging in public policy or building machines that must make moral decisions, like autonomous vehicles. With massively increased opportunities for data collection, improved scientific methods, and more precise insights into human behavior accrued over generations, the complexity and consequence of these ethical quandaries will increase in step with, and may even outpace, our scientific development.

"If we were ever to achieve substantial progress toward our stated aim—toward the understanding, prediction, and control of mental and behavioral phenomena—the implications for every aspect of society would make brave men tremble," George A. Miller, one of the pioneers of the cognitive revolution, wrote presciently in 1969.

A future far from guaranteed

George Miller was similarly prophetic in other ways. "The most urgent problems of our world today are the problems we have made for ourselves," he wrote fifty years ago. "They are human problems whose solutions will require us to change our behavior and our social institutions." The projections that the Earth will remain a suitable home for us only consider the whims of the stars—they do not consider our own influence on our destiny. In assessing the risks to our future, many experts agree that the greatest threats to our well-being and survival are anthropogenic, whether they are related to global war, destructive technology, or environmental disaster.

As we look ahead, our future is marked by both technological power and increasing uncertainty of that power. Behavioral science could serve two key roles in helping ensure that the future we build is one we want to live in. First, insights gleaned from the behavioral sciences can help us design and tune technology to human well-being and thriving—social connection, purpose, and equity. Second, experimental methods can help us evaluate whether our attempts are achieving our aims. And by empirically studying the ways that technological fusion influences our minds and behaviors, research can help us determine how far technology should go, and what boundaries we should keep between us and our creations.

If behavioral science can help us shape these new technologies and our behaviors in light of our values and psychological factors that we know lead to human flourishing, then behavioral science may prove to be as consequential to our future as the technology that will define it. And as we consider such distant horizons, many of the questions we will face tomorrow, we can begin answering today. ∎

Nathaniel Barr is a professor of creativity and creative thinking at Sheridan College and a scientific advisor at BEworks. His primary areas of expertise are cognitive psychology and applied behavioral science. His published works span a wide array of topics, including creativity, innovation, bullshit, belief, the intersection of thinking and technology, and the role of behavioral science in navigating humanity's most pressing challenges.

Kelly Peters is the CEO and cofounder of behavioral science institute and applied research firm BEworks. Her primary interest is in the methodological development of philosophical principles of science to real world application. Throughout her career, she has been a pioneer of innovative technology and business models.

Acknowledgements

The *Behavioral Scientist* editorial team would like to thank the individuals and organizations who helped make Brain Meets World possible.

To our authors, whose original ideas, insights, and experiences fill these pages.

To our individual supporters—patrons, donors, and early supporters—whose financial gifts and encouragement helped bring Brain Meets World to life.

To our organizational partners—founding, supporting, and donors—whose financial backing and belief in the mission allowed us to expand online and in print: ideas42, Behavioral Science & Policy Association, Center for Decision Research, Behavioral Insights Team, The Behavioural Architects, Behavioural Economics in Action at Rotman, Busara, BVA Nudge Consulting, Character Lab, Convergent Behavioral Science Initiative, Irrational Labs, Kahneman-Treisman Center for Behavioral Science & Public Policy, Penn Master of Behavioral and Decision Sciences, Center for Health Incentives & Behavioral Economics, Humu, John Templeton Foundation, Behavior Change for Good, Center for Advanced Hindsight, Evidn, and Rare Center for Behavior & the Environment.

To our advisory board members, for their continuous support and timely advice.

To the design team at Journey Group, including Mike Ryan, Jessica Thier, Jacob Melton, Brittany Fan, Andrew Greeley, and Allison Canter for their good judgment and reliable guidance as we built Brain Meets World.

To you, our reader, whose own ideas and insights will further advance what is in these pages.

Credits

"Utopia" by Wisława Szymborska from *MAP: Collected and Last Poems*, translated from the Polish by Clare Cavanagh and Stanisław Barańczak. English translation Copyright © 2015 by Houghton Mifflin Harcourt. Reprinted by permission of Mariner Books, an imprint of HarperCollins Publishers. All rights reserved.

"An Horatian Notion" by Thomas Lux from *New and Selected Poems: 1975 – 1995*. Copyright © 1997 by Thomas Lux. Reprinted by permission of Mariner Books, an imprint of HarperCollins Publishers. All rights reserved.

Support *Behavioral Scientist*

Support original behavioral science journalism today by making a tax-deductible donation at behavioralscientist.org/donate. For sponsorship inquiries, please email editor@behavioralscientist.org.

Letters to the editor can be sent to editor@behavioralscientist.org.